THE POLICY OF SIMMERING

THE POLICY OF SIMMERING

A STUDY OF BRITISH POLICY
DURING THE SPANISH CIVIL WAR
1936 – 1939

BY

WM. LAIRD KLEINE-AHLBRANDT

WITH A FOREWORD BY

SIR HAROLD MITCHELL

Institute of Hispanic American and Luso-Brazilian Studies
Stanford University

MARTINUS NIJHOFF / THE HAGUE / 1962

TO KEETJE

PRINTED IN THE NETHERLANDS

FOREWORD

Few modern events have aroused more controversy than the Spanish Civil War. This controversy was especially acute in Great Britain, which was torn between its distrust of Nazi Germany and Fascist Italy on the one hand and of Communist Russia on the other. The British public, pacifist in sentiment and determined to avoid war at almost any cost, sensed the danger implicit in the Civil War, yet realised its impotence to control events in Spain which indeed it little understood. The British Government, though under heavy attack from the Opposition and from a handful of its own supporters, succeeded in its endeavours to keep the country out of war on this occasion. The neutrality of Spain, even after Mussolini had entered World War II, was of inestimable value to Britain after the debacle in the summer of 1940. It may be therefore that British policy during the Civil War paid off later on as well as achieving its purpose at the time.

Dr. Kleine's book, lucidly written and carefully documented, examines the British attitude toward the Spanish Civil War. The author has the advantage of belonging to a generation which is able to analyse these events with historical detachment. Yet his understanding and easy style have made the period live.

Neutrality was not easy for Britain. Its far-reaching interests in trading with Spain and in passage through Iberian waters again and again raised awkward problems. These ranged from the sinking of vessels by unidentified submarines to the *Arantzazu Mendi* affair. Opening a House of Commons debate on January 19, 1937, Mr. Anthony Eden defined his government's policy when he said: "there are British interests in this Spanish conflict, and they are two fold. First, that the conflict shall not spread beyond the boundaries of Spain; and second, that the political independence and the territorial integrity of Spain shall be achieved." My own view expressed on that occasion, immediately after my return from a visit to Spain was that: "We should do all that we can to preserve our present efforts for neutrality and still further try to close the frontiers to arms going in." Time has not changed my opinion that the Foreign Secretary's policy was the right one for Great Britain. Each of his objectives was obtained, notwithstanding his resignation before the end of the war.

In retrospect, the Spanish Civil War seems like a prologue to World War II. This book is particularly relevant at a period when not less grave problems from Laos to Berlin face the Western Powers. I commend it as a valuable addition to the literature on the Spanish Civil War and indispensable for the understanding of the British attitude at that time.

HAROLD PATON MITCHELL

Institute of Hispanic American and Luso-Brazilian Studies,
Stanford University
June 1962

PREFACE

For centuries British statesmen have been concerned with problems arising from foreign civil war, which on each occurrence seem to occasion the same questions: What are the war's international implications? How is the balance of power to be affected? If there will be intervention, how should it be handled? What sacrifices should be made and what actions taken? In this respect the Spanish Civil War was little different from others, but to the extent that this dangerously ideological struggle threatened to pull the rest of Europe like a whirlpool into its midst, it marked a departure, if only in extent, from previous situations.

This book purports to study the forces released by that war, investigating how one country, Great Britain, reacted to them. Taking this policy in relation to its times – the actions and motives of other European powers naturally form part of the picture – both sides of the coin are examined: the effect of British action on international affairs and their reverberations, in turn, on domestic politics.

Although British policy in the immediate years before World War II has had extensive treatment, there seems to be a genuine lack when it comes to the question of Spain. In view of the extent to which this war captured the attention of the British people and occupied with tedious negotations their leaders, this lacuna appears surprising; nevertheless it exists. Perhaps the British concentration on isolating the Civil War from other main events of the period has also carried over into historical research, or perhaps it is due to a tendency to lump all British policy under that convenient, disapproving term "appeasement."

Consequently now that there has appeared sufficient material from which to form an appraisal of Britain's course of action, it seems opportune to complete the general picture of those years by analysing in depth this missing link.

The research has been based extensively on primary source material: government documents, memoirs, newspapers, annuals, etc. In addition to British documentation, extensive use has been made of German and American foreign policy papers, which in many instances give inside accounts of British negotiations. The American diplomatic correspondence is particularly valuable in this respect because the detached position that the United States enjoyed in regard to noninterventionist nations permitted her a measure of confidence denied by those countries to each other; this is especially true of Britain and France. The most interesting Italian sources are those of Galeazzo Ciano who describes the character of British diplomacy in her negotiations with his country on Spain and the Mediterranean.

British memoirs, for example those of Hugh Dalton and Leopold Amery, are generally more valuable for the opinions they express than the information they supply; Winston Churchill's account, including the reproduction of pertinent correspondence written with all manner of officialdom in the years he was out of office, is also useful. Very little has been written by Neville Chamberlain; Feiling's biography prints some of his correspondence. The fact that there is even less on Baldwin probably frightens away the biographer who has yet to write the definitive story of his life – even so, perhaps no amount of material will help to explain the man satisfactorily. In the realm of diplomacy there have been some interesting accounts written by men in the Foreign Office, but with the exception of Ciano few of these memoirs give a profound insight into British policy.

Debates of Parliament, the League of Nations, and Labour Conferences have been used with the intention of indicating the essence of a particular debate with its principal issues. *The Survey of International Affairs* and the *Annual Register* are valuable as chronographs, and, although written close to the events they describe, in many simplify research.

Those who have helped me at one stage or another in the preparation of this work, I should like to gratefully acknowledge: to Dr. Jacques Freymond, Director of the *Institut Universitaire de Hautes Etudes Internationales* in Geneva, Professor Maurice Baumont, under whose direction the manuscript was written, and to Professor Louis J. Halle.

USE OF FOOTNOTES

At first reference the title of a documentary source is listed completely; subsequently, and also in the case of memoirs, general works, etc., unless citing an author with more than one work in the bibliography in which case the title is still included, all footnotes appear in abbreviated form. Authors are mentioned by their last names; documents have shortened or abbreviated titles. Thus, Duff Cooper, *Old Men Forget*, p. 214 becomes Cooper, p. 214; the *Survey of International Affairs* is referred to as *Survey;* the *Foreign Relations of the United States* is shortened to *USD*, i.e. United States Documents; *Documents on British Foreign Policy* are *BD; Documents on German Foreign Policy* are *GD; British White Papers* are *Cmd; Soviet Documents on Foreign Policy* are *SD*, etc. Parliamentary debates are referred to in the text by their dates, but in the event that a footnote was held necessary they are cited as *Hansard*. In all cases the complete titles can be found in the bibliography.

TABLE OF CONTENTS

INTRODUCTION

I. THE WORLD OF IMAGINATION

George the Fifth, who for the last quarter century seemed to symbolize Britain's attempt to adjust her tradition to the cold uncertainty following the Great War, died on January 20, 1936. Several days later as the funeral cortège was proceeding to Westminster Hall the caisson carrying the King's body received a sudden jolt which caused a cross on the imperial crown to fall from the coffin. Some people regarded this as a bad omen.

In terms of the happier, more heroic days of Victorianism, the victory of World War I had left Britain an empty responsibility. During the Twenties there was experimentation with internationalism. But after the financial crisis of 1931, Britain became more introspective, concentrating on her internal problems, acknowledging the old concepts of international specialization and economic cooperation to be no longer operative or adequate, or what was worse, desirable. The British democratic birth right, nonchalantly taken for granted, was being threatened by an apparently more dynamic order. The period was marked by crushing unemployment paralyzing whole areas with inactivity. The birth rate decreased while the popularity of gambling soared, a condition no doubt influenced by a feeling that the latter was a less expensive investment in future hope than the former. Nevertheless, as late as 1935 there still existed the belief that the problems of Europe could be solved peacefully. Outside of extreme pacifism or total war, British policy had three prospects: first, there was rearmament coupled with a diminution of international tension by negotiations; second, there could be reliance on collective security backed again by rearmament; and third, a policy of disarmament fostered through the League. The Labour Party preferred the last of these alternatives; the

Government in varying combinations favoured the first two, which led in time to the policy of appeasement.

German Rearmament and Mussolini's aggression in Ethiopia were the major concerns of British statesmen in 1935. In April the British together with the French and the Italians issued a declaration that they were completely agreed in opposing "any unilateral repudiation of treaties which may endanger the peace of Europe." While aiming at Nazi Germany the Stresa Conference conveniently overlooked the intentions of Mussolini. The British Government, not wanting to alienate Mussolini in spite of his colonial ambitions, proposed a deal, and Eden was sent to Rome the third week of June with a plan to buy him off with Ethiopian territorial concessions. Mussolini rudely dismissed the proposals. As the Duce became more bellicose British public opinion became more demanding that their Government stand by her League commitments to prevent the rape of helpless Ethiopia. The result was a half-hearted attempt to apply sanctions, ending with the failure of the League and the estrangement of Mussolini.

Hitler meantime had plans of his own and on March 7, 1936, in direct violation of the Locarno and Versailles treaties and over the opposition of his own General Staff, he marched his army into the demilitarized Rhineland. If there were ever a time to stop Hitler it was then, but nothing happened. France, plagued as usual by indecision, would not act without solid British support and Stanley Baldwin did not feel he had the right to commit Britain. Hitler's *fait accompli* seriously damaged France's Eastern system of security and there seemed to be no desire on the part of Britain to offer her any substitute. Britain's apparent desire to go it alone revived traditional French suspicions of her reliability in time of crisis.

Britain's answer to the increasing menace of armed dictatorship was concentration on rearmament, but even with the realization that she must be strong to protect her democracy, there was hesitation. The Imperial Defense Committee started to plan for the inevitable war, but only when Hitler attacked Poland four years later would their "world of imagination" be transformed into a "world of reality." [1] Lord Ismay recalled making a proposal in 1936 for an augmentation of anti-aircraft artillery to Chamberlain, then Chancelor of the Exchequer, who, preoccupied with economy in Government, remarked "that he was prepared to agree to the additional guns now proposed, but that he sincerely hoped that the last word had been spoken and that there would

---

[1] Ismay, p. 84.

be no further demands." [1] The Prime Minister Stanley Baldwin was essentially a humanist who thought that if the need for a policy or measure was great enough, the public would have it; in what was probably more justification than explanation, he wondered if the British people would march on any other occasion than if they believed their own frontiers to be in danger. In Government circles there was no predisposition for strong action; men of energy were regarded suspiciously. While the Government consisted of tired men who showed no inclination towards experimentation, the Opposition was worse. "In the House of Commons," wrote Robert Bernays, a Liberal M.P., "they exhibit confusion of council and weakness in action. Their back benchers are chafing at what they regard as timidity in leadership, and their front benchers are embarrassed at the feebleness of the debating talent and lack of political sense of those behind them... The majority of them are painstaking elderly trades unionists who can speak with effect on the conditions in their own particular industries, but who lack the power of appreciating great political issues. It is rather pathetic sometimes to see them when some complicated issue is being discussed, sitting row upon row, puzzled and bored, while controversy hurtles above and beyond them." [2]

However pessimistic, this atmosphere was disturbed by signs of change; as early as the previous January (1935) Churchill, returning from abroad, sensed a new mood which could "contemplate war against Fascist or Nazi tyranny." Hitherto smothered in pacifism "the use of force gradually became a decisive point in the minds of a vast mass of peaceloving people." [3]

By July 1936 British foreign policy appeared bankrupt. Collective security was shattered, the League of Nations a dismal failure. Relations with Germany and Italy were at an all time low. Harmony with France was considerably strained. Britain had lost the initiative and only in her complete conversion to a war time psychology three years later would it be regained. Into this atmosphere came the Spanish Civil War.

2. THE CROSS OF THE SPANIARDS

In Spanish culture Britain found much to admire, in her politics practically nothing. For a country purporting constantly to express the

[1] *Ibid.*, p. 80.
[2] *The Fortnightly*, July 1936, p. 37.
[3] Churchill, p. 147.

highest Christian virtues, the reality appeared a shameful hypocrisy; an absence of responsibility, a love for blood sports and a predilection towards revolt had left a legacy of sadism, bigotry, violence and confusion. For over three hundred years the history of Spain has been one of decline, which by virtue of the area's geographic importance encouraged foreign intervention. Realizing the danger of permitting other countries to exploit Spanish weakness, British diplomacy was traditionally designed to keep Spain as neutral and as friendly as possible. Consequently intervention when it occurred had usually been temporary, but because of recurring internal chaos it had usually been frequent.

Oversimplified, Spain's problem has been her difficulty in reconciling an anachronistic medievalism to the demands of modern society. The monarchy as a symbol of unity was so discredited that in 1931 it was effortlessly whisked away. Its replacement had no hold on the average Spaniard's sympathy and was only respected as long as it accorded with self-interest. From the start, the Republic was committed to reform, but too much was attempted at once and too many powerful interests were alienated. The Spanish middle class, insignificant by general European standards, furnished the Republic with its leaders; however, cut off from the illiterate masses and any significant power base, these liberal Democrats were ill equipped to control the emerging disorder. The words *Liberté, Egalité, Fraternité* fell from their lips with distressing ambiguity while the barest levels of personal security were scarcely attainable. To complicate matters, the Republican Constitution was a weak instrument, denying the Government continuing stability necessary to protect it against radical shifts of opinion. As a result reforms undertaken by one coalition were easily nullified by another. There were plots from the Right as well as the Left; terror and violence were inevitable. Seeking to retain abusive privileges, the Right provoked violence on the Left, anxious to settle overnight scores centuries old. Composed of the Army, the Aristocracy and the Catholic Church, the Right was generally more cohesive than the hopelessly disorganized, constantly unreconciled Left whose workers' organizations were mainly divided among Socialists, Communists, Syndicalists and Anarchists. Their Republican loyalty based on suspicion and animosity was sporadic, abusive and of doubtful character. Spain's moderate elements tragically could not command the respect inside their country as they did from without and never were the force they seemed to epitomize. Although intervention affected its general course, the war began because Spain chose to solve her problems in a traditional manner. Salvador de Madariaga wrote that "neither Communism, Russian or otherwise, nor Nazi-Fascism, German or otherwise, had the slightest possibility of provoking a Civil War in 1936, even if they tried, which they did not. Such a power was exclusively in the hands of the army officers and of the Union workers." [1]

But while this evaluation would satisfy an historian, the war's internal causes, although they might have shaped his sympathies, were not the chief concern of the British statesman. Fascist and Nazi and Soviet conspiracies seemed all too real to discount; however, just as the dictator nations were directed toward intervention, Britain was psychologically committed to neutrality. Her role might have encouraged greater intervention, but concerned primarily with the avoidance of war she intentionally preferred abdication to action.

[1] Madariaga, p. 482.

CHAPTER I

FORMULATION OF A POLICY

I. SEARCH

July weather depressing for its lack of sunshine and abundance of rain gave Britain a sombre backdrop for the collapse of Spanish democracy. Although there had been previous reports of terror and confusion it was not until several days before the seventeenth that diplomatic correspondence hinted at the possibility of a *coup d'état*. The early confusion made it difficult to ascertain exact power relationships, but as it was evident that there would be civil war, it was also clear that the war was more than purely Spanish. "It promises to be a bleak and bitter future for the Spanish people," wrote the *Guardian*.[1] Frequently in the past the rivalries of Europe had been fought on Spanish soil, but for the first time it appeared that the rivalries of Spain would be fought on the soil of Europe. Apprehensively Britain temporized. The Rebels were lucky to have timed their revolt for the vacation, said one critic, because the "Englishman on holiday doesn't want to be bothered with foreign wars." [2]

The Spanish Civil war was also badly anticipated by the British Press, only when actual fighting broke out did there come a realization that the summer might bring more exciting news than the Olympic Games. So contradictory and unreliable was news in the early days that the B.B.C. adopted the practice of plainly stating the questionability of their sources, leaving the listener judge its authencity for himself.

Unlike the British, the French attitude evolved rapidly. Léon Blum's government, in power less than two months, was facing its severest challenge. As a coalition of the Left its first reaction was to send the

---

[1] *Manchester Guardian*, July 31, 1936.
[2] *New Statesman and Nation*, August 22, 1936.

Republic aid, and Blum approved a request for the shipment of arms and ammunition. The Communists, the *Confédération Générale du Travail*, and part of Blum's own Socialist Party were in favour of pro-Republican intervention. On the other hand, the French Right, ideologically sympathetic to Franco, was afraid the example of Spanish class warfare would be transferred to their own country. Meanwhile Britain continued to play the Sphinx. On July 22, Charles Corbin, the French Ambassador in London, telephoned Blum to inform him of increasing British anxiety over France's decision to supply arms to the Republic.[1] He urged his chief to come immediately to London for discussions with British heads of state. The next day Blum and his Foreign Minister, Yvon Delbos, flew to the British capital where they heard Anthony Eden's warning of the grave international consequences which could result if France supplied aid to the Madrid government. Eden declared that any French assistance could provoke serious international repercussions with Germany and Italy. According to another account, at luncheon on the 23rd Blum informed the British Foreign Minister that he intented to satisfy a Republican request for arms. Eden reportedly answered, "It is your business, but I ask you one thing. Be careful." [2] At the time it was supposed that the British actually suggested the policy of Non-Intervention and, in order to silence the Labour opposition, desired that policy be proposed by the French Socialists.[3] It is doubtful though that Britain was more specific than proposing general neutrality. (The American Ambassador in Spain, however, felt that Non-Intervention was "hatched in London and that Blum was practically blackmailed into acceptance."[4]) Although naturally concerned about French action, Britain was noticeably at a loss for specific recommendations. When Blum returned home on July 25, he quickly called a Cabinet meeting at which, after a long debate, he with the support of the Radicals Edouard Daladier and Delbos was able to convince his coalition's less moderate elements to unanimously accept a position of neutrality.

Behind Blum's action can be seen the strong hand of Alexis Léger, the Secretary General of the Ministry of Foreign Affairs. It was he who prompted the Premier to meet Eden in London and it is he whom reliable historians [5] credit with the policy of Non-Intervention. Léger

[1] *Foreign Relations of the United States*, 1936, II, pp. 447–449; see also Hull, p. 476.
[2] *Les Evénements Survenus en France 1933–1939*, I, p. 217.
[3] Dell, p. 146.
[4] Bowers, p. 281.
[5] Craig and Gilbert, p. 391; Madariaga, p. 505.

believed that British support could only be insured if France were willing to forego aid to the Republic. French domestic affairs inclined Blum towards Léger's advice. Being the leader of a heterogeneous coalition, the *Front Populaire* (called by the Right the *Front Crapulaire*), Blum would have had to risk his political life over aid to the Republic. Although his sympathies were plain, he was too concerned with domestic social change to run risks in foreign policy. On July 31, Winston Churchill wrote a letter to Ambassador Corbin. "I am sure if France sent airplanes etc. to the present Madrid Government and the Germans pushed in from the the other angle, the dominant forces here would be pleased with Germany and Italy and estranged from France." [1] The future Prime Minister had touched on an habitual fear. The same day, in addressing the Foreign Affairs Committee of the Senate, Blum stated catagorically that future shipments had been forbidden.[2] Non-Intervention was then conceived as a proposition to other Mediterranean powers, namely Britain and Italy, to enter a formal commitment of non-interference in, and supply of arms to, Spain. On August 1, after a particularly stormy session, the Council of Ministers adopted this policy, and immediately took steps to "address an urgent appeal to the principal interested Governments for the immediate adoption and strict observance with regard to Spain of common rules of Non-Intervention." [3]

Britain received the French note on August 2nd and two days later replied favourably, expressing the desire that the plan be extended to all powers who might send arms. But even while sounding out foreign capitals on Non-Intervention France was having second thoughts; Italian and German aid made the implications of a Nationalist victory indeed seem dangerous. When Philip Noel-Baker was in Paris, Blum tried to impress him that Franco could be as menacing to Britain as to France. Being a member of the Opposition Noel-Baker could do no more than suggest he contact the secretary of Baldwin's Cabinet, Sir Maurice Hankey. Acting on this advice Blum sent Admiral Darlan to London.[4] (This action on the part of Blum was indeed strange. Surely he did not need Noel-Baker to advise him where he should go to contact officials of the British Government. Even if it cannot be fully explained, this extremely unorthodox procedure does at least give an insight into the diffidence which must have existed at that time between

---

[1] Churchill, p. 166.
[2] *USD.*, 1936, II, p. 451
[3] *Ibid.*, p. 455.
[4] *Evénements Survenus*, I, p. 219.

Paris and London.) Despite Britain's positive response, Blum's *Chef de Cabinet*, André Blumel, said that their Government "had been rather lukewarm in its support of the French initiative." This, he explained by the attitude of certain Conservative elements which felt "the triumph of the Spanish Government would mean Communism and disorder." [1]

The same week in the Commons Eden tried to clear away any clouds of suspicion of undue British influence on the French Government. "It is suggested," he said "that the French Government took their initiative under strong British pressure... of course there is not a word of truth in that story. It is pure fabrication." [2] Although Labour leaders did support the right of the Republic to buy arms they did not give any evidence of desiring intervention. Arthur Greenwood, Deputy Leader of the Labour party, answered Eden by saying it was common talk in Paris if France were the mother of Non-Intervention at least Great Britain was the father.

The Germans and Italians answered the French note on August 4, identically maintaining that since their countries naturally did not interfere in Spanish internal politics it was quite unnecessary for them to make a formal declaration of neutrality. Hoping to lead by example Britain and France produced formal pledges of Non-Intervention. Britain urged Germany to join in a similar undertaking. It had little effect. The German Foreign Minister, Constantin Von Neurath, replied his country would study the proposal, but said that one had to realize "it was easy to make such an agreement on paper, but extraordinarily difficult to carry... out in practice." The good faith of Russia was questionable and even assuming the best French intentions it would be extremely difficult to seal the long Franco-Spanish frontier.[3] The last remark undoubtedly referred to France's failure to close their frontier to unofficial assistance.

Several days after the French Non-Intervention proposal the British Ambassador in Paris, Sir George Clerk, in an interview with Delbos, warned France that Britain would not consider herself bound by the Locarno agreement if France as a result of arms deliveries to Spain were attacked by Germany.[4] Clerk probably exceeded his instructions, but the point stuck. About the same time Admiral Darlan returned from London, where he had seen his British counterpart, Admiral of the Fleet Lord Chatfield, who had admonished him that French aid to

---

[1] *USD.*, 1936, II, p. 503.
[2] 29 October 1936.
[3] *Documents on German Foreign Policy*, Series D, III, pp. 34–35.
[4] Alvarez dél Vayo, *Freedom's Battle*, p. 68; Dell, p. 147; Bowers, p. 262; Werth, p. 117.

Spain meant British displeasure.[1] On August 8 the French Cabinet in deference to Britain decided to close the Spanish frontier.[2]

While Germany cautiously procrastinated, Mussolini demonstrated more enthusiasm to intervene. Both felt that time would work to Franco's advantage. On August 14 the *Manchester Guardian* correctly said, "one cannot escape the feeling that Italy and Germany are playing for time, waiting to see if the Rebels will win, and if that is so the British and French Governments will be in the unfortunate position of being out maneuvred by their very proper anxiety not to complicate the international situation." [3] Although Germany had little interest allowing the Republic to win, there existed genuine opposition to adventurism and knight-errantry. Army Chief of Staff, General Von Fritsch, agreed to use Spain as a place to blood weapons, but felt that country too awkward strategically for running unnecessary risks.[4] Regarding intervention as a dangerous game, Mussolini showed more anxiety than during the course of the Ethopian war; eventually planning to join Non-Intervention, he wanted to continue arms deliveries as long as possible.[5]

Britain's ambivalence continued to worry the French. Sections of the British population were unenthusiastic about a Republican victory because it would mean a strengthening of Communism; on the other hand a Rebel victory was also undesirable for it would be detrimental to Britain's Mediterranean interests. The United States Ambassador in London, Robert W. Bingham, remarked, "It is perhaps significant that there is no enthusiastic support for either side, but it is generally felt that which ever side wins Spain will be under an extremist government which in either form would present disadvantages in this country." [6] When Sir Robert Vansittart, the Permanent Undersecretary of State for Foreign Affairs, came through Paris on his way home from Berlin, Léon Blum got the impression that the Englishman did not fully realize the dangerous implications of the Spanish situation. Blum felt that this might be due to Vansittart's long absence from London.[7] Negotiations with Italy were another source of disappointment. While Mussolini delayed by insisting prohibition be extended to fund collecting, he emphatically denied he was guided by ulterior motives. Next to these

[1] *Evénements Survenus*, I, p. 219.
[2] Cot, p. 345.
[3] *Guardian*, August 14, 1936.
[4] Liddell-Hart, p. 98.
[5] *GD.*, pp. 38–40.
[6] *USD.*, 1936, II, p. 507.
[7] *Ibid.*, p. 504.

tactics the Germans appeared propitiatory and Paris felt that "there might well be a policy of Germany showing a conciliatory attitude to please the British while the Italians took the brunt of holding up the agreement with comparative evasive tactics." [1]

It is true that at this time Hitler saw no advantage in antagonizing Great Britain. Like Macbeth sounding out Banquo, he did not desire to pass a point of no return. Germany had been disappointed that Britain showed no signs of being swept away in an anti-Communist rampage [2] and she felt, if complications arose over their intervention, that the British Government, together with France and Russia, would support the Republic. Far from convinced the Rebels would win, a feeling which persisted almost until the end of the war, German attitude makes it safe to assume that, had she then faced a determined British policy, she would have backed down, taking Italy with her. At least at this time it does not appear that Germany was willing to treat Spain as a *casus belli* any more than was Britain, although the presence of the larger part of her fleet in Spanish waters did give the impression that she might.

Non-Intervention between Britain and France was formalized on August 15 in identical notes. The two parties "resolved to abstain from all interference, direct or indirect, in the internal affairs" of Spain. Two days later the Germans agreed, followed by Italy on the 21st, and Russia the 23rd. (In all, Non-Intervention declarations were made by twenty-two other nations.) In their note the Germans added that they desired to see governments take steps to prohibit their nationals from participating in the conflict; the Italians made more deceptive qualifications. In raising a question about indirect interference, Italy had neglected to include the very part which pledged rigorous abstention from all interference direct or indirect. Thus their interpretation amounted in fact to an attempt to dictate what others must or must not do without binding herself to prohibit the enrolment of volunteers. The French and British, more concerned in having declarations followed by definite arms embargos, preferred not to interpret this as a reservation. (The Germans, however, had regarded it for what is was. "That the Italian Government has attempted, by the way its reply has been formulated, to reserve far-reaching freedom of action for all contingencies is just as obvious as that it does not intend to abide by the declaration any-

[1] *Ibid.*, p. 502.
[2] *Guardian*, August 7, 1936.

way." [1]) In advance of full commitments from the others, Britain declared a complete embargo. The action of forbidding the export of war materials to Spain together with the support given the French proposal for Non-Intervention seemed to indicate (to André Blumel) Britain was at last showing "a clearer realization of the implications to their interests of a victory of the military rebellion in Spain." [2] On August 24 the situation took an apparent turn for the better: the German Government decided to place an embargo on the export of arms. When joined with similar actions from other countries, it appeared a crisis had been avoided.[3] At the same time conversations were in progress between France and Britain over an Italian proposal which suggested the establishment of a commission to supervise an embargo. "Since it might no doubt be safely assumed that sooner or later accusation would be made against one country or another as having violated the arms embargo, it seemed desirable to the British Government to appoint such a Commission of the powers concerned." [4] The Commission was to serve as a coordinating body for enforcement dealing with all pertinent documents of violations and further negotiations; the word "control" was not mentioned. In spite of the proposed organisation's anemic character, the Germans had misgivings; their first reaction was rejection. They told the British Government that they preferred to inform them directly of matters concerning Non-Intervention instead of becoming involved in a formal committee. In an exchange of notes Britain assured Germany that the function of the committee would be primarily coordination, that "there was no question of setting up the committee in London as an independent body which would have to make decisions or whose jurisdiction might be later extended in any way; it was a question of only organizing loosely the diplomatic representatives of the interested powers." [5] Germany had thus been assured that the Non-Intervention Committee would only be a debating society and, realizing the best way to control the Committee was from the inside, consented to join.

The Non-Intervention Committee reflected rather than created policy; it changed little and revealed less. The record of its meetings lie, unpublished, in the files of the British Foreign Office, still marked

[1] GD., p. 60.
[2] USD., 1936, II, p. 503.
[3] Legislative measures taken by various Governments to enforce Non-Intervention are contained in Cmd. 5300.
[4] GD., p. 57.
[5] Ibid., p. 69.

"confidential." Its sessions were remarkable for their passion: charges, counter-charges, accusations, denials, appeals to cooperation, cutting sarcasm, all were commonplace. The Committee gave Germany and Italy an opportunity for close cooperation; it also isolated Russia. It was never recognized as anything more than secondary diplomacy.[1]

The first meeting took place in the British Foreign Office on September 9, 1936. The first chairman, William S. Morrison, Financial Secretary to the Treasury, was succeeded later in the month by Lord Plymouth, an Under-Secretary of State in the Colonial Office, who by his moderation was the perfect conciliator for the Non-Intervention Committee's warring factions. In the first month the Committee, outside of the question of getting Portugal to join, was concerned mainly with matters pertaining to organization. The scope of the organization became clear with the adoption of the rules of procedure; by limiting complaints only to those countries who actually participated in the accord, the Committee, in effect, "insulated itself against consideration of charges preferred by private individuals, newspaper observers, international organizations, the Madrid Government, the Rebels and governments other than those meeting in London." [2] There were no provisions for publication of reports, for sanctions against violators or provisions for appeal to any other body. After each session the press was handed a communiqué telling of the Committee's progress, but this was restricted by the general tenor of the rules which discouraged as far as possible the presentation of complaints.[3] The full Committee, composed at this moment of twenty six countries, was by its size too unwieldy for effective action; too many foreign offices would have been required to devote too much time to the business of Non-Intervention. The matter was resolved by the formation of a Sub-Committee, limited to the five principal powers plus three lesser ones. (They were Britain, France, Italy, Germany, Russia with Belgium, Czechoslovakia and Sweden; Portugal was added September 28.) It was in this body that all the plans for supervision and control were later formulated. In time the larger committee became merely a ratifying body for decisions already taken; in fact, plenary sessions became increasingly rare as the Sub-Committee assumed full powers. The Non-Intervention Committee was financed through contributions, chiefly from the larger powers; however, delay or refusal of payment was

---

[1] For the general effect of events on Committee affairs see Chronology.
[2] Padelford, pp. 70–71.
[3] *Ibid.*

common, and the necessary funds were invariably supplied by either France or Britain. In view of the conscientious efforts made to stalemate the Committee's work, it is remarkable that anything at all was accomplished. That it was, was due primarily to the efforts of Great Britain, for, in her desire to play the role of mediator, she often went to exasperating lengths to give violators the benefit of the doubt long after the doubt had been removed. Her role, therefore, if not a study in dynamism, is at least one in patience.

2. THE PROBLEMS OF THE OPPOSITION

The British Labour Party was instinctively pro-Republican, but its leaders were too sophisticated to regard the affair as simply a case of sentiment. With many actual and potential divisions in their ranks, their Executive was not anxious to complicate matters by hasty action, and was therefore at first inclined to support Non-Intervention. The dilatory tactics practiced by Germany and Italy, however, had caused a considerable amount of anxiety and on August 26 they sent a deputation to the Foreign Office. Eden and Lord Halifax apparently were able to conciliate them for in coming away they expressed, to the amazement of some, that they were fully satisfied with the efforts being made by the Government. Two days later they reported formally to the Parliamentary Labour Party, the General Council of the Trade Union Congress, and the National Executive, all of which expressed sympathy for the Republic and condemned the breaches of international law. However, they deplored the effect of Non-Intervention on the Republic, and admitted that, if the agreements were applied immediately and loyally observed, they could have a favourable effect on international peace. George Lansbury, former leader of the Labour Party, was in favour of summoning Parliament to consider the imposition of a truce, a move which the First Lord of the Admiralty Sir Samuel Hoare considered pointless and which prompted him to say that the passionate desire of peace seemed to be universal except among the Socialist opposition. "As a rule," he continued, "parties of the Left were pacifists. Our parties of the Left were militarists, but militarists who wanted wars without armies, or air forces." [1] Hoare was too hasty in his criticism: The Labour Party was demanding nothing more than a workable policy of Non-Intervention. The Labour moderates, however,

[1] *Times*, August 27, 1936.

embodying a Fabian perspective, were increasingly coming under attack. The Fabian Society as the home of the intellectual *avant-garde* was being replaced by the Left Book Club, an organization with heavy Marxist overtones. To varying degrees, men like Professor Harold Laski and Sir Richard Stafford Cripps were preaching that Socialism might not be possible without some form of constitutional upheaval; since the 1931 economic collapse they and others inclined more and more to Marxist conceptions of strategy. Divisions over questions of rearmament and Spain were accentuated by differences of ideology. Leaders like Clement Attlee and the Trade Unionist Ernest Bevin felt that Labour, if it ever were going to come to power on its own, must demonstrate to the traditionally conservative mass of the British voter that it could act with responsibility. The British Labour Party had the good fortune of being controlled by moderate, in many cases middle class, intellectuals. The Spanish Civil War, however, posed a threat to this leadership; by reducing issues to dangerous simplicities, it assisted the Party's extremist elements, more concerned with challenging the Executive on shortsighted ideological extremes than working for long range evolutionary objectives. Increase in political adventurism was manifest at all levels; everyone who deplored Fascism, and who didn't, was called to the test. The majority of the Party continued to support their Executive, but the confusion resulting from a division of loyalty considerably impaired Party unity.

During the early part of September the National Council of Labour held a joint meeting; the discussion about Spain created so much confusion that for the first time in several years it was impossible to agree on a resolution to be first debated by the Trade Union Congress and then by the Party Conference. While in session, it was decided to clarify the position of British Labour with that of the French Socialists; [1] a delegation, composed of Hugh Dalton, George Hicks and William Gillies was therefore sent to see Léon Blum. The amount of contact, existing between French politicians of the Left, especially the Socialists, and the leaders of the British Labour Party had been considerable; many personal friendships had their origin in frequent encounters at domestic and international conferences. Léon Blum had the habit of referring to the B.L.P. as "my British comrades." On the other hand, until the beginning of the Civil War, meetings of British Labour leaders with their Spanish counterparts were practically zero, friendship even less. This situation was unfortunate because a sounder

[1] Dalton, pp. 95–96.

knowledge of the Spanish Labour Movement's character might have
made British Labourites less romantic about its aims. At a private
dinner at his house some thirty kilometres outside Paris, Blum, in
emphasizing that Non-Intervention had been his and not Eden's
original proposition, said he was sure that this policy, if fully observed
by all European Governments, would help the Spanish Government
forces much more than the free supply of arms; "even if it was not
fully observed, if there were only comparatively small infractions by
Hitler and Mussolini, it would still be better for our friends in Spain
than opening the floodgates." Blum also admitted that because the
Non-Intervention agreement was not in force, he was still sending
airplanes to Spain. While speaking he looked at his watch and said, yes,
at this very moment "some French aircraft should be arriving." [1]
Labour's action in soliciting support from the chief of state of a foreign
power certainly appears as highly improper behaviour. And indeed its
implications might have proved embarrassing under different circumstances or had the present government been less sophisticated. But in
the latter respect these liberties taken by the British Labour Party were
more tolerated than certainly would have been the case in other more
nationalistic countries.

The annual meeting of the Trade Union Congress was held during
the second week of September (coincidental with that of the Non-Intervention Committee). Customarily the Party holds their convention
several weeks after the T.U.C., whose proceedings are generally considered a dress rehearsal for the parent organization. The leadership of
the Labour Party revolved around an alliance of Clement Attlee and
Ernest Bevin; the one commanding the support of the Parliamentary
and Intellectual sections, the other the T.U.C. Attlee could not have
had a better colleague: matured in Trade Unionism, matter-of-fact,
knowing the mind of the working class like few men, Bevin was one of
the Party's leadings exponents of rearmament; "democracy" he said,
"cannot be protected merely be passing resolutions." [2] On Spain he did
not conceal his dislike for a system of Non-Intervention which prevented the Republican Government from buying the arms necessary
for its own defense, but he thought that "without the general embargo
more arms would go to the insurgents than to the Government; and
that with Germany and Italy actively supporting the insurrection, the
war in Spain would almost inevitably become a general European war."[3]

[1] *Ibid.*
[2] *Times*, September 11, 1936.
[3] *Ibid.*

The General Council of Trade Unions regarded the Government's policy as "distasteful but inevitable," [1] and overwhelming support (3,029,000 to 51,000) given by the delegates for Non-Intervention was a clear defeat for the Unions' extremists.

The rest of September violations of Non-Intervention increased. During the third week the question of the War was ineffectually handled by the League of Nations Assembly, and on the 28th the Spanish Republic published documents showing the extent to which Germany and Italy were violating the agreement. The publication of this dossier made little impression in Geneva, but it had important repercussions in Britain among the ranks of Labour. Embarrassing to the Executives' decision to support the Government, the disclosure of this evidence, on the eve of the Edinburgh Conference, prompted the National Council to declare that it was profoundly impressed by the serious nature of the allegations. Their admission immediately touched off speculation that Labour was reconsidering its policy.[2] The Labour leadership, though unchanged in their belief that effective Non-Intervention was the best policy, now faced the approaching Party conference with a more difficult proposition. To make matters worse, several days before the opening Stafford Cripps launched an extremely vitriolic attack on the Government, denouncing even all efforts of recruitment into the armed forces. Widely covered in the press, Cripps' extremism gave the conference a bad start. "Our annual conference of the Labour Party at Edinburgh in 1936 was a most unhappy experience," Dalton commented. To begin with the conference hall was inadequate and worse, "no smoking was allowed... the exits, to which smokers retreated, were very draughty. The delegates, therefore, were irritable from the start, and many soon caught colds, and coughed and snuffed in hideous chorus." [3] The two chief issues, Spain and rearmament, were impossible to separate; other less dramatic issues were either forgotten or handled haphazardly. (The previous week the Conservative Congress had been held at Margate. Lasting only two days, October 1 and 2, unattended even by the Prime Minister, who did not find it necessary to interrupt his vacation, the Conservatives quickly dispensed with the question of Spain. In paying tribute to Blum's initiative in the present policy, Chamberlain on the second day briefly mentioned the International Committee "which has been set up in London to arrange the

---

[1] *Ibid.*
[2] *New York Times*, October 1, 1936.
[3] Dalton, pp. 97–98.

details of the measures required to enforce the policy of Non-Intervention.") [1]

On the first afternoon of their conference the Labour Executive introduced a resolution supporting a policy of effective Non-Intervention. Arthur Greenwood's defense was very badly received and even when Ernest Bevin spoke, his appeals to party responsibility did little to remove the existing hostility. The resolution was finally carried, but after the first day of debates there appeared so much confusion and contradiction that one reporter wrote, "the Labour Party is left after today's conference an enfeebled political force." [2] The next day, October 6, Spain was again on the agenda; the Executive opened the question of Non-Intervention by submitting a resolution which held "that the violation of a new international undertaking by Germany and Italy must inevitably lead to a reconsideration of the situation by other powers." [3] It was carried by a vote of over three and a half to one, after an extremely determined opposition voiced their disapproval. Aneurin Bevan, the former coalminer from Wales, soundly denouncing the Executive for continuing a policy of Non-Intervention that was leading to the eventual destruction of democracy in Europe, was cheered as he left the rostrum. The climax occurred on Wednesday morning. Isabel de Palencia, a representative from the Spanish Republic [4] of maternal Scottish parentage, speaking fluent English, made an appeal so moving that the whole conference rose to its feet as one and sang "The Red Flag." Palencia received the demonstration motionlessly, greeting the cheers with the clenched fist salute. As soon as the noise subsided delegates started to shout "What about Non-Intervention now?" and immediately "efforts were begun, with influential support, to have the whole Spanish question raised afresh and Monday's vote reversed." [5] In the luncheon recess, it was agreed that Attlee and Greenwood immediately leave the conference for London to discuss, once again, the policy of Non-Intervention directly with the Government.

Since Baldwin was on vacation at Aix-les-Bains, the two men talked to Neville Chamberlain who emphasized the measures taken in the in-

---

[1] *Times*, October 3, 1936.
[2] *Guardian*, October 9, 1936.
[3] *Annual Register*, 1936, p. 83.
[4] Palencia was supposed to directly follow Bevan in speaking order, but due to some mistake she did not have her chance to address the conference until after the resolution had been passed. Whether this mixup was or was not intentional has not been determined. Brome, p. 107.
[5] Dalton, p. 99.

vestigation of violations as proof of the Government's determination to make Non-Intervention work. For the second time Labour leaders appeared reassured. Attlee and Greenwood returned to the conference. On the 5th, the last day, they proposed a further resolution: if Non-Intervention after immediate investigation were discovered to be ineffective or discovered to be definitely violated, the British together with the French would take steps to restore to the Republic their right to buy arms. On the surface it supported Non-Intervention, but Attlee, realizing what was at stake, warned,

> If the Non-Intervention comes to an end, the dangers must be faced by everybody, and we must all be prepared to take responsibility for any decision we come to. We know there are risks. If we demand that the Government of this country should take action to end this agreement, we must be prepared to take any risks which may attend their action. I want that to be absolutely clear.[1]

The Labour Chief had been under great pressure with an almost impossible task of reconciliation. On previous occasions it had appeared that the Labour Party was on the verge of disintegration, but now this feeling was stronger. Attlee faced many things at once; although his resolution on Spain was passed, there was more at stake than a plurality of votes. Attlee apparently was trying to find a policy in harmony with reason, responsibility, and Labour ideology, while at the same time preserving the Party's unity. To be sure, there were men like Herbert Morrison who opposed Non-Intervention but nevertheless could be counted upon for support; but others, like Cripps and Bevan, convinced that the Labour movement was enfeebled, welcomed support from the Communist Party. (The Communists, at their own conference, had just called for a mobilization of the Left, feeling that their aims could best be achieved through the formation of a United Front.) Although Cripps was no longer a member of the Labour Party Executive, he enjoyed a considerable influence among younger party members; on his own he had been conferring directly with the Communist Party in an effort to bring them together with elements in his own party. Under the impetus of Spain a United Front campaign was launched. The Labour hierarchy had neither now, nor at any other time, found reason to profit by such an association. They were extremely reluctant during the course of the Spanish War to take part in any mass campaigns. No matter how much public sympathy might be attached to one cause or another, the fear of being faced with Communist infiltration with its undesirable connotations kept them for the most part aloof.

[1] *Ibid.*, p. 100.

During the Spanish Civil War they made it extremely clear that, although pro-Republican, they would never tolerate totalitarianism from the Left any more than they would from the Right. Sympathy was not completely unanimous, though; Hugh Dalton wrote: "I was not an admirer of the Spanish approximation to democracy. When the Spanish Left lost the elections in 1934, they started an armed revolt to reverse the result of the voting. This was very inefficient and soon fizzled out. Now that the Spanish Right had lost in 1936, they too had started an armed revolt which looked more serious. I did not think well of this political method." Dalton admitted his personal views were not shared by a majority of his colleagues and for this reason he tended to refrain from speaking on the subject in Parliament.[1]

The 1936 Party Congress, the most important to be held during the Civil War, was a test to see how far Labour could be influenced by her Left wing elements. The key bloc of votes lay with the Trade Unions and it was their support for Attlee which determined the issue. Harold Laski, active in the Socialist League, after the Edinburgh Conference closed, complained bitterly "those blasted trade unions decided on Non-Intervention though they knew this meant a sure Rebel victory in Spain. They turned down all and every suggestion for a united front; and they made the foreign policy debates at Edinburgh the worst mess since 1931." [2] Because of the hostility he incurred for his views on the unification of the Left, Laski one time put his chances for Party expulsion at five to one. (Cripps, slightly worse, was twenty to one.)

In time though, most of those who agreed with Laski's position either submitted quietly to Party policy or discredited themselves by their very emotion. This widely exalted minority, divorcing themselves from the consequence of their agitation had, according to Dalton, "no clue in their minds to the risks, and the realities, for Britain of a general war. Nor did they, even dimly, comprehend how unrepresentative they were, on this issue, of the great mass of their fellow countrymen." [3] Attlee had tried as best he could to paper the cracks of Labour disharmony, but finally was forced to conclude that, although renegades against party discipline be prominent and middle class, there was no reason why they should be treated any differently from the rank and file. The showdown with the diehards on the United Front issue was to come at the 1937 Party Conference.

[1] *Ibid.*, p. 96.
[2] Martin, p. 105.
[3] Dalton, p. 100.

In spite of the embarrassment caused by Labour's Left Wing, the resultant problems being of a different nature were more easily solved than the other important question provoked by the Civil War: how far was the desire to stand up to the dictators compatible with opposition to military spending? The paradox between pacifism and rearmament was one that divided families as well as parties. It seemed no longer possible to simply dismiss the apparent contradiction as did one reporter. "I see no intellectual difficulty in at once working for the victory of the Spanish people and in being glad of the growing pacifist movement in England." [1] Notwithstanding a desire for clarification, the fact remained that by the 1936 Party Conference there existed no clear cut definition. On the second day of debates a resolution was put that defensive forces should be maintained "as are consistent with our country as a member of the League of Nations"; [2] but this ambiguous compromise solved nothing, and only emphasized the Executive's difficulty in reaching agreement. Dalton stated:

I find it difficult in logic to believe that the Labour Party Conference can support unilateral non-rearmament in a world where all are increasing their armaments. [3]

But the opposite point of view, if one were already inclined in that direction, could make just as much sense. George Lansbury said:

Today is no time for going back to the old ideas of force; we must bring even the dictator nations round the table and challenge them not with the might of our arms, but with the might of our reason and common sense. [4]

That not many Labourites were prepared to commit themselves one way or another caused a desert of hesitancy and weakness which had to be passed before approaching a plane of resolution. In observing the Labour Party of this period one is constantly reminded of its indecision; the members naturally felt that their party once in power could produce more responsible government than was possible under the Conservatives, but this is an academic conjecture. What, it is fair to ask, would have been their solution to these matters, if they had had their opportunity? In view of the existing divisions, it is extremely difficult to see that they had any clear alternative, and lacking that, it is therefore impossible to be convinced that Labour could have offered any effective solution for the Spanish crisis. Even though they shared

[1] *New Statesman*, August 22, 1936.
[2] *Labour Party Annual Conference Report*, 1936, p. 182.
[3] *Ibid.*, pp. 184–185.
[4] *Ibid.*, p. 187.

the sympathy of the general British public, they were unable to turn it much to their advantage.

In reality the British people were more pro-Republican than pro-Nationalist. Although savagery was by no means uncommon to both sides, under Franco it seemed to be more organized and deliberate. For this reason the image of a valiant Spanish democracy being eaten by the wolves of Fascism seemed to be generally accepted. But as the war continued and fanaticism, so out of tune with British character, still filled the reports from Spain, the British, if anything, became more convinced that they must remain withdrawn from such a bloody struggle.

To feel sorry for the bull at a Corrida is one thing; it is quite another to jump into the ring. Their feelings for Non-Intervention were consequently strengthened. Among the British intellectuals the Spanish Civil War was a time for self-justification; they were almost unanimously pro-Loyalist. Their protests against the policy of the Government filled the "letters to the editors" columns through out the whole period. For example, an open letter printed in the *New Statesman* early in the war publically expressed "sympathy with the Spanish Government and people and [hoped] that our own government will take every legitimate apportunity of pursuing towards such a foreign government the traditional British policy of sympathetic benevolence." [1] Included in the list of signatures were the names of G. D. H. Cole, E. M. Forster, G. P. Gooch, G. B. S. Haldane, Julian Huxley, David Low, H. G. Wells, Virginia Woolf and Ralph Vaughn Williams.

But among the intellectuals as well as the mass, the minority by determination or extremism seemed to set the general attitude. Paradoxically pacifists often clamored most for direct intervention. As Professor Mowat wrote," the war widened existing divisions, between government and opposition, between right and left (terms hardly used in the political sense in England before this); it brought bitterness and class-consciousness into foreign policy, and so into domestic politics, to an extent unknown before." [2]

It was this splitting, fragmentation of public opinion, which made the war, perhaps more so than the international hazards, such a source of danger to the British way of life.

[1] *New Statesman*, August 22, 1936.
[2] Mowat, p. 577.

CHAPTER II

METAMORPHOSIS OF NON-INTERVENTION

I. SUPPORT WITHDRAWN

In Spain things looked increasingly bad for the Republic. General Franco, confident of victory, expressed his gratitude for the valuable moral and material help which Hitler had given him, and he voiced the hope that he would soon be able to hoist his banner of civilization next to the one already raised in Germany. The encirclement of Madrid, together with Non-Intervention violations, worried the Russians. The Soviet *Chargé d'Affaires* in London stressed in the Non-Intervention Committee that unless violations were immediately discontinued, Russia would consider herself absolved of all obligations arising under the agreement.[1] She received no satisfaction. At one session at which violations were discussed, the Italian representative "after having energetically refuted and repudiated every single point of the allegations directed against Italy, declared that all these allegations were entirely fantastic and devoid of any foundation whatsoever"; [2] Lord Plymouth denied the Soviet request to continue the discussion at a further meeting on the grounds there was lack of evidence that the agreement was being violated. Rumors started that the Soviets were planning to leave the Committee. "Indeed it is hard to believe," said the *Times*, "that the Soviet Government however much they agree with Lord Plymouth's attitude would immediately repudiate their engagements and abandon the neutrality which they have undertaken to observe." [3]

On October 19, influenced by the same events which had motivated the Russians, Attlee wrote a letter to Prime Minister Baldwin in which

---

[1] *Soviet Documents on Foreign Policy*, III, p. 212.
[2] *Guardian*, October 22, 1936.
[3] *Times*, October 20, 1936.

he called for an immediate summoning of Parliament; he said that even though there was no absolute proof there was strong evidence of violation and further delay would only permit further abuse. Baldwin did not see how things could be changed by calling Parliament several days earlier than it was scheduled to meet. Attlee formally reported his correspondence, previously published in the *Times*, to the National Council of Labour, which held on October 22 a discussion on Spain. It was decided that, although the onesided observance of Non-Intervention was deplorable, it was impossible for them to act unilaterally; therefore, common action with the International Federation of Trade Unions and the Labour and Socialist International was proposed. A meeting took place in Paris four days later. The British delegation included Walter Citrine, General Secretary of the T.U.C., who presided, and Arthur Greenwood. The conference unanimously adopted a resolution emphasizing their general disappointment with Non-Intervention, calling upon the British and French Governments to reach an agreement whereby complete commercial liberty would be restored to Republican Spain. Attlee hoped to induce the French Socialists also to abandon Non-Intervention. But Blum had his own irons in the fire. In a previous discussion he had told Hugh Dalton that if the way were opened for general intervention, he would face a very serious internal problem. A general mobilization over a confused quarrel in Spain would mean that he would have to rearm the *Cagoulards*, French "Fascists," who were a direct threat to French democracy.[1] Attlee was disappointed; "the French attitude," he wrote, "hampered us in bringing pressure to bear on our own Government." [2] Herbert Morrison recalls the difficulty in reaching any agreement, "In conversations with French Socialists during this period, which I sought in the hopes of developing an entente about support for the Spanish Republicans which could influence the appeasers, I was disturbed to find that the French Popular Front was afraid for its life. France was so riddled with schism that Blum dared not officially approve intervention." [3]

The meeting of the Labour Executive in London on the 28th endorsed a foregone conclusion: a resolution passed to restore the Republic her customary rights dropped Labour's qualified support of Non-Intervention.[4] What did this mean? It certainly did not mean that

---

[1] Dalton, pp. 95–96.

[2] Attlee, p. 93.

[3] Morrison, pp. 165–166.

[4] In spite of all the lose talk about the Spanish Government's right to buy arms, it should be noted that there is no international law which obliges a country to sell.

Labour leaders were interested in intervention. Far from it. Members of the Party who did favour such a policy were forced to find their support among renegades, Communists, or not at all, with the result that interventionism, when expressed, became less organized and more indefinite. The slogan "arms for Spain," adopted at the meeting on the 28th, clearly implied opposition to Non-Intervention without particularizing in terms of intervention. Labour demanded the Government account for their actions, but outside of a demand to bring policy into line with international law, they offered little. Labour, as well as Conservatives, failed to realize a necessity for firmness on issues of which Spain was only a part. Labour by virtue of their sympathies tended to concentrate too much on the Iberian peninsula, the Government, ironically, not enough.

* * *

Parliament had not met since the end of July and in that recess much had transpired. Labour had gone from support, to qualification, to opposition; the Government from optimism to disappointment. The Spanish debate on the 29th of October seemed to contain all the frustration of the previous months. The Government's position was exposed by Anthony Eden: "Our purpose in this," he said, "was not to help one side or another, but to prevent civil war... from passing the boundaries of Spain and involving the whole of Europe in its orbit." There was no alternative to Non-Intervention than to allow the free export of arms to both sides. "If you can find a better policy, do so." Greenwood spoke for the Opposition: I am aware, he said, that Spanish politics are not like a Mayfair tea party, but still the constitutional government of that country, the Republic, when faced with an armed rebellion, is entitled to purchase the arms necessary to defend herself. As for violations, although they are difficult to prove,[1] could one ignore the reports of all responsible journalists? Even if five percent of their reports are true is it not correct to assume that Non-Intervention has been seriously violated? "Spain has become a pawn in the game of power politics... But had the boot been on the other foot, had there been a Fascist Government faced with a popular revolt from a Popular Front of the Left, would anybody have suggested the policy of Non-Intervention? It would never have been suggested." (There is little

[1] This Government contention can only be judged as a deliberate misrepresentation. Her diplomats in Spain would have had to be blind not to observe the wholesale violations· In Seville for example the Germans were so obvious that their consul there complained to the Foreign Ministry. *GD.*, p. 38.

doubt that Greenwood was right). Labour had never fully given their support to Non-Intervention, but they felt that if it existed it would have to be made effective; the principle in operation had violated all British concepts of fair play and was a complete sham.

I think that in the interests not merely of democracy in Spain, but of the moral authority of international law in Europe and in the World, we should return to the policy of taking international law as our basis and restore to the Spanish people the rights of which they were unfairly robbed.

The debate closed with a speech from the Prime Minister. Baldwin, aroused the previous week from his customary inertia by the King's intention to marry an American divorcee, showed no particular enthusiasm in discussing Spanish affairs. But the activity engendered by the domestic issue seemed to sustain him. His approach, perhaps a bit condescending, was free, nevertheless, from vilification. Reducing the whole matter to very "common language" Baldwin said it was simply a question of Intervention or Non-Intervention. He conceded infractions but thought they had not been of sufficient importance to cause the Government to modify their policy. "If there are some leaks in a dam," he said, "it may at any rate keep the water out for the time being, and you may stop the leaks. It is a very different thing from sweeping away that dam altogether." [1] Baldwin's chief concern was the effect of ideological extremism on the British people. Reminded of the wars of religion and the break-up of the Roman Empire, he revealed thoughts that motivated his foreign policy. With the birth of Communism on the one hand and Fascism on the other there was now

on either side large bodies of men who are prepared to fight and to die for an abstract creed. That is ... far the most dangerous thing in this world today. Therefore we have got in this country, with all that we have to preserve, to take jolly good care that neither of them takes possession of it, because I believe that the preservation of democracy is of such value to the world.

Baldwin was not a great Prime Minister, but in playing down the war's potential divisions he rendered his country a great service.

The same themes would be heard again; surprising for their similarity were the debates on Spain. The same opinions, the same reactions, the same accusations, considerably dulled outside interest in Parliamentary affairs. The average Englishman remained insular; he read "his daily paper, after first glancing at the result of the Test

[1] The French, with a similar metaphor, looked upon the Non-Intervention Committee as a brake, which "undoubtedly slips frequently but which nevertheless has the great merit of serving to keep the situation from plunging precipitately towards a catastrophe." (*USD.*, 1936, II, p. 596.)

Match, of national upheavals, large scale massacres, and civil wars, and then [went] off unconcernedly to his work or his golf." [1] The Conservatives, with no danger of a Cabinet crisis, could discount the attacks of Labour. The die hard Tories and big industrialists, disposed to Franco, were controlled by the Party's moderates, who helped to strengthen rational elements in the Opposition. Fire eating elements on both sides were thus discredited. From the start the Government made her goals plain. According to Eden, the

main immediate concern is that the conflict unfortunately raging in that country should be confined within the narrowest possible limits, in the hope it may be brought to a speedy end. This attitude is in conformity with the deep interest we feel in the maintenance of the integrity of Spain and Spanish possessions. For I need perhaps hardly say that it is a consideration of great moment to us that when Spain emerges from her present troubles that integrity should remain intact and unmenaced from any quarter.[2]

2. FURTHER COMPLICATIONS

Mussolini, sensing the Republic's imminent collapse, started making plans for recognition to concur with the fall of Madrid. Britain also felt the end was near. A high official of the Foreign Office told the American Ambassador that the British, realizing Madrid's capitulation would certainly be followed by German and Italian recognition with all its unpleasant connotations, felt it essential "for the Governments of the democratic countries to take some early action which will prevent Franco from falling into the pockets of Berlin and Rome." [3] As a first step Britain was carefully studying the question of recognition, but personally, he thought, some "middle ground" short of actual recognition could be found to handle the situation. In Rome, Mussolini was showing impatience; although Madrid had not been captured, feeling he might be left out of the spoils if he waited too long, the Duce urged the Germans to join him in sending representatives to Burgos anyway. The Germans, not as restless, advised that no steps be taken until the city's actual surrender. But the Republic's intention to prevent shipping from reaching Rebel ports caused them to change their mind, and on November 18, in agreement with the Italian Government, they announced formal recognition; claiming that the Republic could no

[1] *The Fortnightly*, April 1937, p. 499.
[2] Eden, p. 120.
[3] *USD.*, 1936, II, pp. 550–551.

longer protect German nationals and that effective control of the country had passed to Franco, Hitler decreed that henceforth all future publications refer to the Insurgents as the Spanish National Government, and the Loyalists as the Spanish Bolshevists. The British reacted by reaffirming their policy of Non-Intervention, but the realization that Hitler and Mussolini were now staking their reputation on Franco's victory was not ignored; no people knew better than the British the importance of prestige. The *Manchester Guardian* commented that this recognition "will of course, be a great moral help to the rebels. Will it be followed by increased material help from Germany and Italy? There can be little doubt that it will." [1]

Meanwhile another chain of events caused the British further concern. The Russians, using dummy import-export concerns, had since August been furnishing military supplies to the Republic; at the same time acting through the local Communist party organizations, they had begun a recruitment of volunteers. This activity had hitherto been conducted in an atmosphere of secrecy but on October 23, Russia, admitting her determination to intervene, informed the Non-Intervention Committee that, since violations had created a privileged position for the Insurgents, she would not consider herself bound by the agreement to any greater extent than the other participants.[2] Consequently, during the next few weeks, there was a steady flow of material and manpower to the Madrid front, where in the early days of November it was instrumental in the city's successful defense.

With victory thus retarded, Franco decided to press an attack elsewhere. He chose Catalonia. Planning to use a conventional strategy of encirclement, be announced a blockade of all Eastern ports in Republican hands. By this act Franco directly raised the question of belligerent rights and put British shipping into a dangerous position. Both the Republic and the Insurgents had now blockaded each other by proclamation. When this act had been announced by the Republic during the second week of August, Britain took the position that the imposed blockade had no validity since it could not be considered effective. Franco's case was more ambiguous for the British were not sure whether the Rebel chief's declaration could even be considered as an intention of undertaking an effective blockade in fact. They assumed that his words constituted a general warning to neutral shipping which would enable him to deal more forcefully with Russian

---

[1] *Guardian*, November 20, 1936.
[2] *SD.*, pp. 212–213.

intervention, but Franco certainly did not have sufficient naval strength to meet the requirements of international law. In any case, Britain was interested in finding a quick and uncomplicated solution and since she did not expect to recognize belligerency (she might have, had it not been for French opposition), she had two courses of action: either she would permit the Insurgent Government to interfere with her shipping on the high seas, or she must contemplate the use of force, if necessary, to prevent it.[1] Britain previously had not tolerated any exercise of belligerent rights by either party in Spain. Although serving primarily her own interests and only incidentally those of international law, she was not unaware of the situation's absurdity. A Foreign Office official said "Great Britain and France were recognizing a government no longer in power, Italy and Germany had recognized one that has not come to power, and none of the governments has recognized the real situation, namely, a state of belligerency arising out of the Civil War." [2] In any case, the problem was regarded with enough urgency to merit a special Cabinet meeting on Sunday, November the 22nd. Eden announced their decision the next day in the Commons,

His Majesty's Government have not so far accorded belligerent rights at sea to either side in the Spanish struggle, and they have no present intention of according such rights. As a consequence, His Majesty's ships will, should it prove necessary, protect British merchant ships on the high seas against interference by the ships of either party engaged in the conflict in Spain outside the three mile limit.

This policy solved nothing and pleased nobody. Whatever may be the political reasons which have prompted the present policy, wrote Professor Herbert A. Smith, "I feel sure that in the long run logic and reason can never be disregarded with impunity... [Therefore] in the light of our present knowledge I can only say that I feel grave doubts whether any temporary advantage can in the long run outweigh the harm which is done by the disregard of well tried principles. My hope is that future lawyers will be able to regard the policy pursued in this war as an anomaly. My fear is that future politicians will regard it as a precedent." [3] The Insurgents claimed that it interfered with their

[1] According to the law of nations "A government or régime whose belligerent rights had been recognized by the governments of other countries might exercise the right to visit and search on the high seas ships flying the flags of those countries; but in cases where belligerency was not recognized an attempt to interfere with foreign shipping outside territorial waters might legitimately be resisted by force." *Survey of International Affairs*, 1937, II, p. 258.
[2] *USD.*, 1936, II, p. 574.
[3] *British Year Book of International Law*, 1937, pp. 30–31.

blockade operations, the Republic felt that by warning ships to respect the blockade it gave the Insurgents a status in International Law. In addition Eden said that the Government was going to introduce legislation which would make it a criminal offense for any British vessel to carry arms from foreign ports to any port in Spain. At the same time, not wanting to challenge any potential blockade, Britain asked the Rebels to delimit a safety zone in the Barcelona shipping lanes, where neutral ships would not be exposed to attack. The answer first received was unsatisfactory; repeating her inquiry, Britain was finally informed that foreign neutral shipping would be able to anchor in the port of Barcelona between certain clearly stated geographical quadrants.

The Merchant Shipping (Carriage of Munitions to Spain) Bill, introduced November 27, increasing the effectiveness of Non-Intervention, was principally designed to remove any excuses for Spanish warships to interfere with United Kingdom shipping. According to its provisions all ships registered in the U.K., any colony, protectorate, mandated territory, India, or Newfoundland were under its jurisdiction (The fact that it did not extend to the Commonwealth raised doubts among the Opposition, but the Government rightly maintained that it was not their duty to legislate for that area). In the debate, lasting ten hours, on December 1, Labour held that, while restraining the British carriage of arms, this legislation constituted an act of intervention against the Republic because it did not propose any agreement with the countries aiding Franco. Labour's principal speaker, Philip Noel-Baker, was jeered by a Conservative critic for giving a "gunrunners" lament. A press report observed that "the opposition was significant because the Labour Party gave the impression throughout that what they now wanted was intervention on the side of the Madrid Government, because it was a Left Wing Government." [1] Labour strongly resisted the Government contention that the bill was just another logical step in the policy of Non-Intervention.

In practice, unilateral measures of this type produced negative results. Although only two other countries (Norway and Poland) immediately followed the British lead on the transportation of munitions, almost all the countries, including Germany, Italy and Russia, in the Non-Intervention Agreement had promulgated legislation for its enforcement. Obviously more depended upon the willingness of the authorities charged with administration than upon the integrity of the printed text. For, no matter how much faith is expressed in such

---

[1] *Times*, December 2, 1936.

measures to improve dangerous situations, unless there exists reciprocity, there is bound to be disappointment.

3. THE LEAGUE OF NATIONS IGNORED

Up to this point the League of Nations has been left in the background. In part this omission is understandable for the Non-Intervention Agreement by its very nature insured that most of the questions pertaining to the Civil War would be handled in London, not Geneva. By itself, however, this fact does ignore the subject's further aspect: the role of domination played by Great Britain. Of three Great Powers which remained in the League only Britain was in a position to effectively exploit that organization for her own interests. (Largely as a result of desertion and default; France, as Eden had learned during the Ethiopian affair, was not disposed to assume any initiative, preferring to follow British judgment; Russia, mistrusted, was isolated and ignored. Italy, it was true, was still technically a member of the League, but for some time had refused all participation). But, it should be said, even this one power control, though not conductive to the longevity of an international institution was still more a symptom of the already existing decadence than a cause.

Long before people heard of a general named Franco, there existed in Britain a tendency to use the League as a "smoke screen behind which the diplomaticists, and especially the British Foreign Office could conceal from the public the fact that they had no foreign policy at all. When pressed on the subject by inconvenient people who wanted to know, they could always make their retreat into a mist of platitudes about their firm belief in this great human experiment entirely devoted to the improvement of international relations and to the promotion of the peace, progress and welfare of mankind." [1] Therefore, it is not surprising that a noticeable discrepancy arose between public platitude and achievement. Stanley Baldwin, realizing that the British public was hopelessly infected with Leagomania, was careful to give an impression of benevolence even though it was clear he thought otherwise. Explaining why the Government disregarded the League on the Spanish issue, he said,

[1] Cooper, p. 157.

In the League itself today there are running those same currents of antago-
nistic creeds that are causing us so much trouble in the world, and I do not
honestly know what the League should have done.[1]

Lord Robert Cecil felt that the tendency of the British Government
to avoid bringing important issues to the League was based on the
absence of Germany, Italy and Japan, which made vigorous action impossible. (If anything though, the absence of these obstructionist
powers should have had the opposite effect). On the other hand certain
writers tend to find the key to British action in the existence of the
Commonwealth; according to one [2] British hesitancy lay in the Commonwealth's geographical and constitutional position which made it impossible for her to adopt a firm political line. (While it would be
impossible to deny this explanation partial validity, it is difficult to see
how the Commonwealth, divided on policy among its members, could
have pressured a determined Britain). British action was in reality
fundamentally related to her traditional habit of regarding the League
as an instrument of diplomacy, and when this main purpose could no
longer be advantageously realized, disregard followed inevitably. Chamberlain expressed this idea as Prime Minister, "the League is not
an end in itself, it is a means towards an end, and if the League is
temporarily unable to fulfill its function... what is the use of repeating
parrot-like that we are believers in the League?" [3] Britain was by no
means the only country with this attitude. Ironically most resistance
to her policy came from inside the U.K., not from other members of the
League. The general attitude of other governments for the support of
the League in the struggle for peace was shown quite graphically by
their cavalier treatment of the International Peace Campaign. Headed
by Lord Cecil this organization, strongly influenced by the international situation provoked by the Civil War, sought to arouse international
public opinion to support a return to League diplomacy. On October
1st, an invitation, somewhat grudgingly extended, enabled Cecil to
speak in the Geneva Assembly Hall. Since there was no obligation to
attend, the meeting became a test of interest. Although all other
committee activity was suspended, the meeting was attended by only
104 delegations out of 240 (among the absent, Great Britain and Spain),
the public benches were two thirds empty, the press gallery practically
deserted and Cecil's appeal for the education of public opinion to

[1] 29 October, 1936, *Hansard*, 316, Col. 145.
[2] Charvet, p. 131.
[3] In the Commons, 21 October 1937.

strengthen the League's work for peace was met with indifference.

The question of the War could not be silenced indefinitely and Spanish appeals, although troublesome, could not be dismissed. At the outset, statements of faith and assurances of success tended to silence Spain, but continued violations made impossible the confinement of discussion to a Committee on which the Republic was not represented. The opening of the 17th League Assembly session on 21 September 1936 found Britain apprehensive. Having persistently discouraged heretofore any suggestion that the war should be dealt with by either the Assembly or the Council, the British felt that if they could not actually prevent Spain from speaking they should at least try to control what she might say. At first they suggested that the "President should stop any reference to the subject in the general debate"; [1] but later holding this impossible, they made efforts to persuade directly the Spanish representative, Alvarez Del Vayo, to keep his speech moderate so as to provoke no controversy,[2] and they succesfully advised him not to raise the question formally. When finally he spoke, Alvarez did appear restrained; pleading for a better understanding of his country's moral and legal position and speaking in general terms, he called Non-Intervention contrary to international law and to the advantage of the Rebels. The Assembly listened, but passed no resolution, seeming generally content to let the matter be handled in London.

Dissatisfied with this mild approach, the Spanish delegation three days later, on September 28, made public a series of dispatches which their government had sent earlier to Non-Intervention powers. The League Secretary-General Joseph Avenol, with the approval of France and Britain, had previously refused to publish this material as League documents unless they were submitted as a formal appeal for League intervention. The notes in substance demanded that the embargo on the sale of arms to the Republic be removed and that aid to the Rebels be stopped; they also contained detailed documentation of German and Italian intervention. Meanwhile, the recognition of the Insurgent Government by Germany and Italy the third week in October gave the Republic a solid reason upon which to demand formal League consideration of the war. Their appeal under the terms of Article 11 requested a special session to examine German and Italian acts, which were claimed to constitute virtual aggression against Spain. The British Foreign Office regarded this as an attempt to use the League as a forum

[1] Walters, II, p. 721.
[2] *USD.*, 1936, II, p. 533.

to focus world attention and was worried that the Republicans might try to set up a special League Committee.[1] Spain was perfectly within her right to attempt both, but the British Government had no desire to have League action extend beyond what had already been done at the 17th Assembly. Therefore, first, in order to counteract any propaganda trick that the Republic might play, on December 3rd Britain and France tried counter strategy with an agreement to approach various interested governments to ask cooperation in checking the war. This action, not given much chance of success, was decided mainly because Britain and France were "anxious for their own records that such an action should be taken especially before the meeting of the Council on December 10." [2] Extending beyond a mere desire for propaganda, Britain hoped to solve the Spanish affair by promoting a stalemate. The situation seemed to indicate that the dictators would be favourable and she consequently had no desire to spoil her chances by an unpleasant League session. Officials were far from pleased at the prospect of attending a council meeting and even Russia's Litvinov was said to be furious at the Republic for calling this special session against his advice. Britain's decision not to be represented by her foreign minister was, with the exception of Spain and Sweden, generally observed. This was taken as the Council's desire to be as little involved in the Civil War as possible. Certain countries resented the Anglo-French trick which confused the Council meeting with mediation proposals; it was felt that such public disregard constituted an open affront to League authority.[3]

The unwanted meeting sat from December 10th to 12th. On the 11th, speaking of the disadvantage created for his country, Alvarez del Vayo gave Non-Intervention a sharp critique; he condemned the aid given by Italy and by the "blond Moors," and said sarcastically that it was possible to conceive the final result of this crisis to be "a Europe wholly pacified because all problems and all difficulties would have been settled, thanks to the decisive action of international Fascism." [4] The British delegate, Lord Cranborne, Under Secretary of State for Foreign Affairs, critical of the violators of Non-Intervention and alarmed at the threats to international peace, said vaguely that if the Council could do anything to help end the conflict these meetings would not have been in vain; he expressed his confidence that inter-

[1] USD., 1936, II, p. 586.
[2] Ibid.
[3] Ibid., pp. 607–608.
[4] League of Nations Official Journal, January 1937, p. 8

ventionists would ultimately realize their responsibility and cooperate in measures to make Non-Intervention effective. In referring to the Anglo-French mediation proposal, Cranborne said that

during the last few days, conversations have been proceeding between (France and Britain) with a view to putting an end to the armed conflict in Spain by means of an offer of mediation ... The conception in the minds of the two Governments has been that certain interested nations should make an approach to the two parties with a view, as a first stage, to the negotiation of an armistice. With this object, the Governments of France and the United Kingdom have approached the Governments of Germany, Italy, the Union of Societ Socialist Republics and Portugal, and have asked them to take part in this initiative ... His Majesty's Government is confident that they will realize the very real responsibility which rests on them in this matter.[1]

He called on the Council to bless Britain in her effort and finished his speech with a discussion of international humanitarianism. With few exceptions there was no desire to continue with an examination of Spain's appeal. The Council, composed for the most part of nations already a party to Non-Intervention, simply was content to affirm the obligation of every state not to interfere in the internal affairs of another, urging that the members of the League who were represented on the London Committee spare no pains to make their undertakings as effective as possible. It noted and praised the attempts made by Britain and France for the termination of the conflict, and thereby parroted British desires completely.

The Spanish Foreign Minister could have hardly expected any more but Alvarez Del Vayo in recalling his attitude said, "I was full of hope and impatience to expound to the world the justice of the Spanish cause and the infamy of Fascist aggression, and to abolish the fraud of Non-Intervention." [2] Hopes and intentions, however, were beside the point for it was the British fear of giving Germany and Italy an excuse to withdraw from the Non-Intervention Committee, to cause any atmosphere unfavourable to her other negotiations, which governed this as well as future situations.

* * *

Lacking in vigour, British policy conceded unsolicited opportunities to Germany and Italy. During the war's first six weeks, there was convincing evidence that both Hitler and Mussolini, expecting Britain to adopt a strong position, did not contemplate an active policy of intervention. Neither Baldwin nor the British people however were pre-

[1] *Ibid.*, p. 12.
[2] *The Last Optimist*, pp. 298–299.

pared to run risks; the question whether Hitler or Mussolini would go to war over Spain was never tested. Britain reacted to the ambiguities of the situation by inflexibly increasing her commitment to Non-Intervention. She thus encouraged the dictators to believe in her decadence. Hitler, with advisors like Ribbentrop, came to believe that Britain's decline permitted Germany freedom of action in Europe. Mussolini confirmed similar suspicions. He discovered, for example, that for twenty four million women there were twenty two million men and there were twenty million citizens over the age of fifty, the age limit for men in condition to make war. The dynamism of youth being therefore submerged in a static majority, British society preferred a quiet life, compromise, and peace.[1]

In the first months of Civil War the pattern for future events was established, and neither the position of Labour nor the position of the Government was to change significantly. For immediate needs British efforts were concentrated in two directions. First, feeling that neither side was in a position to win without further assistance, especially manpower, the British Government reasoned that if she could obtain an agreement prohibiting volunteers while enforcing the one against material, the Spanish conflict might reach a *status quo* whereby the Spaniards could arrange their own affairs. By this elaborate bit of wishful thinking, assuming all nations were equally desirous in limiting the war, Britain felt two birds could be had with one stone: the war would subdue, the faces of the dictators would be saved.

Second, but most important, Britain wanted to resolve her differences with Italy. The Ethiopian war had not only deteriorated relations between the two countries, but, destroying the assumption of inviolable naval and aerial preponderance, provoked a re-evaluation of Britain's entire Mediterranean position. If the British were already pessimistic about their capabilities, Mussolini's actions in Spain gave them no cause for insouciance. From the beginning of the war Mussolini had virtually occupied Majorca: whole army divisions were fighting for Franco and air bases were being constructed from Lybia to the Dodecanese. Faced with the prospect that Mussolini was using the Civil War as a medium to challenge their position, the British Government, without the disingenuous hope in a solution from the London Committee, took a more direct approach in defending her endangered interests, and the Mediterranean, so enflamed by the war, largely set the tone for future action, increasing in importance as the war continued.

---

[1] Ciano, *Journal Politique*, p. 24.

CHAPTER III

CONFLICT OF INTERESTS

I. A VITAL ARTERY

A British dispute with Mussolini seemed unavoidable. A certain Raphael had predicted ten years before: "We may look for a resurrection of the mailed fist and blood and iron policies in the Mediterranean" for Mussolini's "successes are likely to lead him on to folly and his crowning piece of egotism will be to cross the powers of England and of France, for his Saturn is" in conflict with "Britain's star Aldebaron, while..." etc. [1] A less celestial explanation can be found in the discongruity of British position and Italian aspirations. British interest in the Mediterranean was both strategic and commercial. Responsible for about twenty percent of all food and raw material imports, (almost entirely those of tin, rubber, and petroleum) the Mediterranean, as a way of transit, involved roughly three fourths of the population and half the land area of the Empire-Commonwealth. With defense resting on an assumption of unrestricted movement, British naval forces could serve a double utility: a means of exerting diplomatic pressure in times of peace and direct force during war. They additionally formed part of the outer defense perimeter for the Home Fleet. To guarantee supply and communication, Britain had established a series of well located naval bases – the most important at either end. In addition to a powerful flotilla, British security depended on the weakness and neutrality of surrounding countries; this was especially true in the case of Gibraltar and Suez where it would have taken active land control by some other power to be threatening. With Italian intervention amounting to expeditionary forces in active occupation of certain areas, the threat in Spain was obvious. As Liddell-Hart later wrote "the one direction in which neither France nor Britain

[1] *Ephemeris of the Planet's Place*, 1927, p. 41 (pamphlet).

can afford to accept the risk of ... concessions is in the Western Mediterranean... Thus from a strategical point of view, the political outcome of the present civil war has the closest bearing on the security of both France and Great Britain, slow as some of their leaders have been to see it. A friendly Spain is desirable; a neutral Spain is vital." [1]

Of all the countries bordering the Mediterranean, certainly Italy from a geographical standpoint alone had the strongest reasons for good relations with Britain. Ninety percent of her imports came by sea; with four and a half times more coast than land frontiers Italy was essentially maritime and should have regarded British naval supremacy with sobriety. Mussolini, however, determined to make Italy great in his life time, felt humiliated as a prisoner in his own lake. He wanted to remake his country in his own image; internally he was hampered by the bourgeoisie, externally by the British. Italy must be a nation of warriors, a combination of Georges Sorel and Ancient Rome. "When the war in Spain is over," he said, "I shall find something else; the Italian character has to be formed through fighting." [2] But Mussolini was no complete fool. He might have wrongly assumed, because Britain appeared reluctant to endanger her fleet for anything other than actual homeland defense, that he was in a position to dominate the Mediterranean, but he did manage to capitalize on the British passion for bargaining; by keeping his prices high he robbed without discouraging the customer. British statesmen contributed to his success. After becoming Prime Minister, Chamberlain wrote "the dictators are too often regarded as though they were entirely inhuman. I believe this idea to be quite erroneous. It is indeed the human side of the dictators which makes them dangerous, but on the other hand, it is this side on which they can be approached with the greatest hope of successful issue." [3]

Negotiations with Italy began modestly. In the fall of 1936 conversations took place to settle minor commercial differences. Italy, upon whose initiative the talks were held, gave the impression that she was anxious to balance her position and the British Foreign Office, feeling that the talks might eventually lead to a more important agenda, had them deliberately protracted. An important exchange occurred on September 12. As a result of Italian occupation in the Balearics, the British *Chargé d'Affaires* in Rome had warned Count Galeazzo Ciano of

---

[1] *Yale Review*, December 1938, pp. 240–241.
[2] Morelli, p. 136.
[3] Feiling, p. 324.

British opposition to any change in the *status quo*. The Italian Foreign Minister was conciliatory; Italy, he said, was innocent of such intention and no treaty with Franco had taken place considering such alteration. Later Ciano repeated these assurances verbally to Eden, but at the time no further problems were pursued; the next move was left to Mussolini.

On November 1, the Duce unexpectedly expressed a desire for better relations, declaring in a speech at Milan that a bilateral conflict between Britain and Italy was unthinkable. The Mediterranean, he said, while for Britain only a "short cut," was for Italy her very life but Italy had no desire to cut this route and only wanted "a sincere, rapid, and complete understanding on the basis of the recognition of reciprocal interests." [1] Mussolini offered nothing new, his words were rather indefinite and, although Britain wanted relations to improve, she was unimpressed. The *Times* thought no agreement could have added anything to Italian rights and interests.[2] The Foreign Office preferred to wait for further details. Two days later Halifax in a speech in the House of Lords denied that, from the British point of view, there had ever existed a difference with Italy. We are always willing, he said, to renew friendly relations which have been a tradition between our countries; there is no need to dwell on whose interests are more concerned, it is sufficient to say that they are complementary. On the same day Ward Price, the *Daily Express* correspondent, interviewed Mussolini. Price relates that he asked Mussolini if he could suggest any practical means to give a concrete form to the friendly overtures which had been made from both sides. Mussolini replied in English, "a gentleman's agreement." Does his Excellency have in mind any concrete agreement defining spheres of influence or non-aggression? The Duce, with an impatient gesture, "There [has] been too much of the pactomania lately. I don't want to increase it. What I should like is something simple and clear, of the kind that both the Fascist and the British temperament appreciate." [3]

On November 5th, Eden emphasized that the Mediterranean could be used to the mutual advantage of both countries, but not merely as a short cut, for to England it was a vital artery. Mussolini replied three days later. Using the official newpaper *Giorno d'Italia*, he said the British statesmen, in corresponding to his speech in Milan, approached

[1] *Times*, November 2, 1936.
[2] *Ibid.*
[3] Price, p. 245.

the spirit of Italian foreign politics. Italy was not a country inclined to bear a grudge; once Ethiopia has been conquered, there was no future policy intended which would be aimed at the legitimate interests of Great Britain. No reference was made publicly for the next six weeks. On December 16, when Eden was asked Italy's commitments on the Balearics, he revealed the conversations which had transpired the previous September. His resumé was more a reminder to the Italians of previous pledges than an intention to enlighten the Commons; Eden emphasized the indivisibility of Mediterranean and Spanish problems.

Meanwhile at the diplomatic level Britain over the past month and a half exhibited considerable willingness to resolve certain embarrassing issues. After the signature of a trade agreement on November 6, Britain gave in effect *de facto* recognition of Italy's Ethiopian conquest (she reduced the status of her Embassy at Addis Ababa to a Consulate.); later she promised not to carry out a proposed strengthening of her Mediterranean fleet. As the year came to an end an accord was produced. Very general in nature and recognizing the compatibility of interests, it was designed from the British standpoint to offer a base upon which a more comprehensive agreement could be built. On December 29, in showing a draft of the proposed declaration to Phillips, the American Ambassador in Italy, the British Embassy expressed "the opinion that the conclusion of this accord will create a favourable atmosphere in which it may be possible to work out a more satisfactory arrangement as regards Spain." The British gave the impression that with the subsequent amelioration of relations they anticipated Mussolini would be more willing to play a responsible part in the fulfillment of Non-Intervention.[1]

Since there was no mention of Spain in the preliminary drafts, the British Ambassador, Sir Eric Drummond, on December 31 specifically requested formal confirmation of Italy's intention to respect Spanish territorial integrity. Ciano replied, "So far as Italy is concerned, the integrity of the present territories of Spain shall in all circumstances remain intact and unmodified."[2] The formal signing took place on January 2, 1937 at the Italian Foreign Ministry, Palazzo Chigi. In the text the two countries promised to "recognize that the freedom of entry into and exit from and transit through, the Mediterranean is a vital interest both to the different parts of the British Empire and Italy;"[3] they undertook to respect each others interests. This was

[1] *USD.*, 1936, II, p. 618.
[2] *GD.*, p. 199.
[3] *Cmd.* 5348.

undefined. They promised not to modify the *status quo*. Also undefined.

In spite of its emphasis on psychological good will, initial expectations lessened considerably when it was learned that immediately prior to January 2 Italy had landed several thousand troops at the port of Cadiz. The Italians claimed, and within the limit of the written text were right, that this in no way affected the agreement. Supporting this contention, Ciano sent Drummond a copy of the agreement accompanied by an explanatory letter in which from the Italian standpoint the entire field of Spanish relations was discussed. According to Ciano this exposé answered "implicitly all the possible questions and inquiries which might eventually arise in Anglo-Italian relations as a result of the Spanish conflict." [1] Britain reacted to the shipment of troops with only mild surprise, (she felt Germany a greater menace in Spain) but forced by public opinion she adopted a "grave view of the Italian action." On January 19th, in defending the Gentleman's Agreement before the Commons Eden said there was no doubt "that this declaration has been of service to appeasement in the Mediterranean."

But if we are to believe him on a later occasion, Eden felt all along that Italy was untrustworthy; in February 1938 he said:

In January last year, after difficult negotiations, we signed the Anglo-Italian Agreement, but within a very few days, indeed almost simultaneously, the first considerable consignment of Italians left for Spain. It may be held that this was not a breach of the letter of our understanding, but no one, I think, surely will contend that it did not run counter to its spirit.

Eden's dislike of Mussolini was no secret; at the time of the Ethiopian affair Mussolini had so purposely and intentionally insulted him in public that Eden probably never forgot it.[2] The atmosphere was different at Rome; Drummond earned Ciano's praise as a man who had come to understand and even like Fascism.[3] Neither attitude successfully countered Mussolini's intervention.

2. PROHIBITION AND CONTROL

After wasting the first three critical months in fruitless attempts to establish the guilt of violations, the Non-Intervention Committee turned to the subject which would occupy its sessions for the duration

[1] *Ciano's Diplomatic Papers*, p. 173.
[2] Cerruti, pp. 281–282.
[3] Ciano, *Journal Politique*, p. 323.

of the War. On December 2, the Chairman's Sub-Committee, acting on a Russian initiative, agreed to examine the question of volunteers while at the same time deciding that Britain send a plan of supervision, previously discussed and approved, to the Spanish Governments.

Britain, working through as well as outside the Committee, issued on December 9 a communiqué reinforcing the diplomacy of the Foreign Office towards renunciation (by Germany, Portugal, Italy and Russia) of all "direct or indirect action which might in any way be calculated to lead to foreign intervention in the conflict"; [1] she envisaged a solution in three stages: strict control of arms and foreign manpower, conclusion of an armistice between Loyalists and Rebels, establishment of a plebiscite enabling the Spaniards to chose their form of government. The Non-Intervention Committee meetings on December 22 and 23, showed how difficult were any prospects towards their implementation.

To begin with, the Spaniards themselves showed no partlcular willingness to comply. Franco's reply to the British note concerning supervision made it clear without open rejection that outside control was unacceptable; the Loyalists accepted the plan in principle, but nevertheless submitted significant reservations. The question of volunteers showed no progress. Germany maintained it was an essential component of the whole issue of indirect intervention and as such was impossible to be considered apart from questions of propaganda, national subscriptions, and political agitation. The Committee was heading for a deadlock and Britain decided to approach the governments directly. On December 26, in cooperation with the French Government, she instructed her embassies in Rome, Berlin, Lisbon and Moscow to encourage individually the necessary steps to end the dispatch of volunteers. The Soviet Government replied favourably within several days but, in spite of the British insistence that "this question is by far the most important and urgent of all those arising out of the war in Spain" [2], the others delayed.

After receiving the *démarche,* Germany and Italy had gone into immediate consultation. Germany suggested they express astonishment that Britain should consider it necessary to appeal for a second time outside the procedure of the London Committee. On December 31 Von Neurath, the German Foreign Minister, told Sir Eric Phipps, the British Ambassador in Berlin, that his country would soon have their

[1] *Guardian,* December 11, 1936.
[2] *GD.,* p. 184.

reply; he said Germany was prepared to join in all measures of localizing the conflict, but that under no circumstances would she tolerate "the establishment of a Soviet Communist government in Spain. Under certain circumstances [she] would even prevent this by force." [1] Neurath had the impression that Britain was definitely pro-Republican and was pushing for a halt of foreign troops because she felt the Loyalist Government, if not faced with a reinforced France, would hold the lead. (On the other hand Claude Bowers, the American Ambassador to Spain, said that most of his colleagues with whom he had talked "cynically comment that England has been forced to the cognizance of the appearance here in great numbers of soldiers from the armies of Germany and Italy, but that nothing will be done to stop the influx of these soldiers").[2]

During the next week British attention was focused elsewhere, but on January 6 the Foreign Office, most likely provoked by adverse criticism of the Gentleman's Agreement, informed the Germans that they were extremely anxious to have an answer within the next few days. Their dispatch expressed "the gravest view of any further prolongation of the present circumstances in which so-called 'volunteers' continue to flow in organized contingents into the affected areas in Spain." [3] The next day Eden made it clear that Germany was mistaken if she assumed that Britain, because of the recent agreement with Italy, was any less interested in reaching agreement or prohibition; in fact, the feeling was to the contrary, for since the Gentleman's Agreement Britain's attitude had considerably stiffened. The Germans felt uncomfortable under these promptings; they informed Phipps that they considered them both regrettable and superfluous and feared that if they were to react favourably it might give the German public the impression that they had done so under British pressure. In Rome on the morning of January 7th Ciano had a discussion with the British Ambassador in which he expressed Mussolini's wish that he was prepared to go to great lengths to avoid future complications and to work for the withdrawal of troops if it were reciprocal. "The conversation ended in a mutual expression of desire to cooperate wholeheartedly in the interests of peace and that the recent British Italian Mediterranean accord was after all the foundation upon which the two Governments could work closely in general matters of European peace." [4]

[1] *Ibid.*, p. 197.
[2] *USD.*, 1937, I, p. 224.
[3] *GD.*, p. 204.
[4] *USD.*, 1937, I, pp. 216–217.

That afternoon the British Foreign Office received the replies. In their memorandum Germany stressed halting of volunteers could only be approved if accompanied by effective guarantees: adoption by other countries, solution of indirect intervention, and execution of embargo control measures. The problem of volunteers was referred back to the London Committee. The Italian note was basically the same but it went so far as to suggest that their soldiers were in Spain because of their hatred of Bolshevism, not government pressure. The German note was harsh and polemical, but Britain forced herself to be conciliatory. Eager to reach an agreement she resorted to an old diplomatic practice; she simply overlooked the German and Italian reservations, noting that there was sufficient general agreement among the powers to take immediate steps to stop the inflow of volunteers. (Giving an impression that there is agreement where it does not exist, is characteristic of politics backed with insufficient force. Britain had tried the same gambit with "success" in regards to the birth of Non-Intervention.) In a note of January 10 Britain elaborated her propositions; she favoured an extension of the Non-Intervention control scheme, going beyond supervision at frontiers and ports to include land and sea approaches. Britain urged each government to pass in advance of negotiations necessary legislation for prohibition; and as affirmation of her good faith, she announced her readiness to apply the Foreign Enlistment Act to Spain, making it an offence for her nationals to volunteer. By unilateral action Britain no doubt hoped, as she had on a previous occasion, to set an example.

The German and Italians did not plan to answer until they had an opportunity to discuss in detail their Spanish commitment. Mussolini had originally invited German participation at a high level staff meeting for January 10th; as he was desirous to bring about "a real decision in Spain" he wanted somebody sent who would have full powers. He suggested Admiral Canaris, but the Germans decided to send no less a personage than Field Marshall Hermann Wilhelm Göring, and what had started as another staff discussion became a personal *tête à tête*.

Meanwhile Britain was becoming anxious; on January 11, Drummond handed Ciano the latest note on the question of volunteers. The British Ambassador said that while waiting a reply, his country had instructed him to find out whether Italy "would be willing to prohibit henceforward the departure of new contingents of volunteers, in view of the fact that the recent disembarkation at Cadiz had produced a deep impression." [1] Ciano replied evasively; he said that it was not Italy's intention to authorize further departures, but it was impossible to make any commitment of the nature requested. He did *not* say that at that moment Italy was preparing to send more troops to participate in a surprise attack against the city of Malaga.

Parliament reconvened on the 19th. In a general appraisal of the international situation the Foreign Secretary claimed thatal, though intervention would definitely prolong the conflict, the risk of war had been clearly diminished. It was erroneous to believe the outcome would mean a foreign power were going to dominate the internal and external affairs of Spain. In the long run Britain stood to gain because, "the great mass of the proud Spanish people will feel the least ill will to those nations which intervened the least." Attlee was more concerned with the present; he accused Eden of turning the ban on volunteers into a gesture in the hope the Fascists would be inspired by his example. "We believe in democracy," said he, "but if democracy is to survive it must be prepared to stand up to the dictators." The adverse effect which the Government's recent plan on volunteers had on Loyalists convinced Labour that the Conservatives, anticipating the eventual victory of Franco, were only concerned with the preservation of British financial interests. But although Labour tended to ignore the disappearance of democracy in the Spanish Republic, they had no belief that there was more democracy in Communism than Fascism. In this debate they continually stressed the threats to Britain's position in the Mediterranean, the threats to the independance of Spain, and the threats to traditional concepts of humanitarianism; both sides of the House produced arguments about the legal status of volunteers, the freedom of Spanish elections, the question of law and order and public opinion. The House was divided chiefly on the basis of fear. The Government did not lean toward Franco out of affection, they feared his alternative. The Labour Party feared Fascism more than their attraction to the Spanish Republic, strong though that it was. The greater adjudged danger, whether from the extreme Right or extreme Left, thus determined the sides but the prejudicial orientation of both parties made all support appear positive.

Göring, having arrived at Rome on January 13, was in the meantime making the rounds of Italian officialdom, always magnificently dressed in his own self-styled uniforms. His visit with Crown Prince

---

[1] *Ciano's Diplomatic Papers*, p. 79.

Umberto on the 18th was followed by a three day rest at Capri, after which he returned to Rome for a final meeting with Mussolini. The conversations which took place on the evening of January 23 at the Palazzo Venezia are more important because of what they revealed and confirmed than of what they concretely accomplished. Both countries were playing a double game, freely admitted to each other, in which they individually sought a rapprochement with Britain, while strengthening relations with each other. Most of the talk concerned policy toward Britain and Spain. Mussolini found it disgusting that Britain should always mask her political objectives by offering economic concessions. Eden's speech of the 19th (in which he had re-emphasized that the Mediterranean was "not a short cut, but an important main road") had left Mussolini in a bad humour and he solicited German help to put Britain in her place. Göring conceded that advice from England was of no interest for his country, that British objectives must not be allowed to stand in the way of German and Italian interests in Spain, but that Germany "intends to go only to the limits of what is possible, thus preventing a general war from developing from the complications in Spain." [1] Mussolini agreed but had said that the Spanish situation had to be resolved in accordance with their political ideals. They should continue to cooperate, reaffirm their desire for peace while perfecting their armament.

On the specific problem of volunteers the situation was regarded favourably. Without a general embargo, Italy would continue to send troops; with an embargo, there would be little disadvantage, for there already existed enough troops in Spain to assure a Rebel victory. Mussolini did not believe a war was possible in 1937; "Léon Blum and his collaborators wish to avoid it... England, too, fears a general conflict, and Russia will certainly not let things go beyond the limit." [2] Göring cautioned it would be well to treat English public opinion with respect, feeling that the English Conservatives could be exploited through their fear of Bolshevism – a task best left to Germany, since it would be "rather difficult for Italy to convince the English Conservatives in view of the events in the Mediterranean." Göring then called attention to the distinction between the true English Conservatives, with whom Germany was seeking a *modus vivendi*, and the Government proper, which was composed of Left Wing elements; there was great sympathy for Germany among the English common people, but

[1] *Ibid.*, p. 85.
[2] *Ibid.*, p. 86.

the Foreign Office "whether for idealistic reasons or on grounds of tradition maintains a position of absolute hostility to Germany. Moreover, a further obstacle to Anglo-German collaboration is to be found in the strong influence of Freemasons and Jews in the British Empire." [1] Near the end of the conversation Göring on Hitler's behalf invited Mussolini to visit Germany (accepted at once) and after a short discussion on Austria and some words of appreciation he bid the Duce farewell and departed for Berlin.

Two days later Germany and Italy replied to Britain's note (of January 10), informing her that necessary legislation, already prepared to prevent the departure of volunteers, would be enforced as soon as similar measures had been adopted by others and as soon as the London Committee had agreed on a means of control. To return to the Committee meant of course a return to verbal sabotage, but Britain, encouraged, submitted (on January 29) a control scheme which provided for "naval patrols off Spanish ports to stop shipments of munitions to both sides" and "military observers along the frontiers to report movements of foreign 'volunteer' troops." [2] In spite of the limitations of Germany and Italy and the rejection of Portugal, Britain persisted, thinking the best solution lay in measures governments were willing adopt locally; she had no desire to effect control by imposing a blockade, for enforcement involved the very dangers she was eager to avoid.

The situation changed somewhat by February 8th. Jubilant at the capitulation of Malaga, which convinced them of Franco's final triumph, the Italians appeared more cooperative. They would support future prohibitions of volunteers but they were flatly opposed to any British counter move to evacuate those already there. Still, this was a beginning and on February 10 a special Sub-Committee (comprising Britain, France, Germany, Italy, Portugal and the Soviet Union) began to juggle previously unacceptable proposals to iron out differences. The work was finished six days later. (The only objector, Portugal, came to an special agreement under British pressure.) The new plan contained three features; a scheme of supervision, a naval patrol, and a coordinating committee. The Spanish frontier was placed under international observers, stationed at ports, along boundaries or on board ships. These inspectors though had no power beyond investigation of complaints, examination of cargos and notification of

---

[1] *Ibid.*, p. 87.
[2] *New York Times*, January 30, 1937.

violations. The naval patrol was entrusted to the four main powers, (Germany, Italy, Britain, and France) who were each responsible for a certain patrol area. In general, Britain and France (with the exception of a British patrol on the Basque coast) were assigned to that coastline controlled by the Rebels, the Germans and Italians to that of the Loyalists. The Soviet Union and Portugal had been originally invited to take part in the patrol. But the U.S.S.R., dissatisfied with what she had been offered (the Bay of Biscay), withdrew in favour of Britain or France. At the same time Portugal took similar action, deferring to Germany or Italy. Primarily functions were limited to observation but, when necessary, patrol vessels were authorized to stop, board, examine the registry certificate and clearance papers of any ship, ascertain whether observing officers were on board or whether the vessel had stopped at an observation post before approaching Spanish waters." [1] The International Body, responsible directly to the Non-Intervention Committee, would receive reports and organize over-all operation. It was not possible, however, to make these plans operational by the specified dates, as the Committee had had to devote considerable time and energy to preliminary arrangements. Accordingly, although the naval patrol had started on March the 13th, the final plan, including supervision of land frontiers, did not take effect until the 19th of April, and by that time much had changed. But it was clear even before, that the scheme would not work.

3. UNFULFILLED DESIRES

The control scheme was unsuccessful because determination of violation was greater than that of enforcement. The agreement had no standing or guarantee other than the good faith of its members and as in Non-Intervention itself, any power was at liberty to withdraw for "reasons of state." Since patrol vessels had no right to stop non-participating ships evasion was relatively easy. One could send, for example, a shipment of prohibited materials to a non-participating state where the cargo could be transferred to that country's ships, or a ship could be supplied with the flags and registry of a non-participating country.

Mussolini had formalized control in a mood of triumph. But success and moods are fickle, and the capture of Malaga was followed by a

---

[1] Padelford, pp. 84–85.

military disaster. Mussolini had hoped to make the Guadalajara offensive the turning point of the war; he had committed three Black Shirt divisions, but in the ensuing route he not only lost the General Luizzi, but his reputation as well. Of the men captured there was something absurdly pathetic: some Italian prisoners claimed they had no idea they were being shipped to Spain, saying that they had enlisted to fight in Ethopia for a dollar a day. Mussolini tried to dismiss the reverse as inconsequential and temporary. Determined even more to seek a victory, he blamed the Spanish for the defeat. But Guadalajara revealed the true nature of the Italian warror. The German General Thoma observed from his experiences in Spain that the Italians were bad fighters because they disliked noise.[1] The blow to Italian prestige was discussed openly among the Insurgents who, already resenting Mussolini's condescending attitude and the open sneers of the Italian Foreign Legionnaires, welcomed the humiliation with satisfaction.[2] On another level, Mussolini's defeat destroyed any hope Britain had for effecting voluntary foreign troop withdrawals. She realized Mussolini would now seek to recover his prestige. If, for example, the soldiers in Spain were not reinforced, they might be either killed or captured, producing so serious a blow to the Duce's authority that his regime could topple. The possibility of further Italian intervention was discussed on March the 25th in a conference between Sir George Clerk and Yvon Delbos. They discussed the advisability of adopting firm naval control measures in the event Mussolini broke with the Non-Intervention agreement and tried to send further troops. The French felt the British were not prepared to accept the risks posed by such action. Realizing the difficult situation in which Mussolini was placed, the French Government was willing to forget the past and work for effective future prohibition, but they, as well as the British, were frankly unable to see any solution.[3] Russia, on the other hand, was not disposed to consider Mussolini's pride. Litvinov sensed that internal conditions in Italy made the present extremely favourable for firmness; if Mussolini were served notice that any further transfers of manpower would not be tolerated, they would not take place.[4]

The British leaders manifested no desire to follow this advice; they hoped that Mussolini might be induced to negotiate a direct improvement of relations. Moreover, realizing a decisive victory by either side

[1] Liddell-Hart, p. 165.
[2] *USD.*, 1937, I, p. 269.
[3] *Ibid.*, p. 261.
[4] *Ibid.*, p. 261.

in Spain could disturb the balance of power, they preferred a peace without victory. Although the Non-Intervention Committee had been unsuccessful in many instances, nevertheless the war had been contained and a certain equilibrium maintained. In spite of the apparent axis between Mussolini and Hitler, Britain did not dismiss the possibility of neutralizing its effects. Especially with Italy there appeared no major difficulty which could not be settled to mutual satisfaction. Britain tended to minimize the long term effects of intervention, but just as the war seemed to reach more manageable proportions it was entering its most dangerous phase.

Internally, the spring of 1937 was notorious for probably the strongest crisis of opinion during the Civil War. The wilful destruction of Guernica, the sacred city of the Basques, on April 26, left the average Briton with feelings of horror and disgust. As townspeople were doing their marketing a fleet of Junker and Heinkel bombers pounded Guernica for three and a half hours until it was practically levelled. The *Times* correspondent in Bilbao called the raid unparalleled in military history: "Guernica was not a military objective, it lay far behind the lines. The object of the bombardment was seemingly the demoralization of the civil population and the destruction of the cradle of the Basque race." [1] Franco tried to shift blame on to the Bolshevists, but denials were futile. The correspondent of the *Star* was an actual eye witness; three others, from the *Times*, Reuter's, and *Daily Express*, arrived shortly after the attack; all their reports were in basic agreement. Public opinion was immediately arroused. A British clergyman wrote: "If a European war comes, as seems all too likely, the scenes in Guernica will be repeated in every big town in Europe." [2] In both houses of Parliament indignation demanded action. Of all the protagonists in the Civil War the most admirable to the British mind were the Basques, strongly religious, proud of their localism, hostile to Franco, uncorrupted by either Communism or Fascism. Eden said that the Government deeply deplored the bombing of civilians in Spain and would work for agreements ending this practice. However, outside of promising to join an inquiry and to continue efforts to make the war more humane, he could not commit himself. Even Attlee called for only a collective protest. Later though, supported by public opinion, the British Government arranged for the transfer of four thousand Basque children to Southampton. The

[1] *Times*, May 6, 1937.
[2] *Guardian*, May 7, 1937.

whole operation was carried out under the protection of the Royal Navy. Accustomed as we are today to wholesale shifts of populations, these measures might be regarded as insignificant; in their day, however, they were quite remarkable. As important as this single act of charity was, it was only a part of a larger effort on the part of the British to ameliorate the condition of the Spanish people by diminishing some of the war's most ruthless side effects.

There were of course the Government's attempts to humanize the war, notably in protesting the bombing of open cities and promoting prisoner of war exchanges; the British Embassy in Madrid resembled a refugee center during the, war but results on the unofficial level were more impressive. Concerned primarily with direct aid and assistance, organizations sprang up, extremely heterogenous in character. Their mission could be general relief, like the Friends of Spain or the National Joint Committee for Spanish Relief, or they could be confined to more specialized tasks, like the London Committee for Spanish Medical Aid or the Basque Children's Committee. They could be national, or regional and local. Committees, for example, were established in various cities and districts (Merseyside, Tyneside, Manchester, Yorkshire, London and Bristol) to collect funds to send shiploads of wheat to Spain; this undertaking was handled on a more national scale by the Churches Foodship Appeal. The International Solidarity Fund of the International Federation of Trade Unions was used for sending direct aid to Spanish workers. In the course of the war the National Council, as a result of frequent appeals, was able to raise £53,000; a Milk for Spain Fund sent £22,000 worth of milk to the Republic. Also sent were various consignments of clothes, tobacco and soap. Separate Unions assumed special tasks, eg. the Mine Workers Federation started a fund of £23,000 to help the orphans of the miners of the Asturias.[1] In general, assistance went more to the Republican side and came not only from Labour supporters but from Conservatives and Liberals as well. Unfortunately however, this British charity did nothing to modify the war's bloody course which at the moment was making it impossible for the Government to continue to regard the Spanish theater as one divorced from other European affairs.

[1] *Annual Labour Report*, 1938, pp. 5–10.

CHAPTER IV

CHANGE OF LEADERSHIP

I. DEFENSE OF INTERESTS

Giving Italy and Germany a monopoly of surveillance over the Loyalist coast had been a mistake. Tension increased as their gunboats under the cover of darkness roamed the area shelling Republican towns. At the same time, pressing his attack on Bilbao, Franco boldly declared a blockade of the Bay of Biscay, seeking by force to prevent all ships, including those with food stuffs, from reaching Republican destination. In a period of four days (April 6–10) a total of four ships were stopped. In advance of any specific orders from the Cabinet the British Admiralty had informed all British merchantmen within the area to proceed to St. Jean de Luz to await instruction. When it was learned that Franco intended to enforce his determination by planting mines, Baldwin called a special meeting of the Cabinet, at which (on April 10) it was decided ships would only be protected on the high seas; they were warned to avoid risks against which it was impossible to give protection. Two days later Baldwin said the British would not tolerate any interference with British shipping at sea, but he did not assure that ships carrying food to Bilbao through the blockade, even though it was unrecognized as such, would get protection; he firmly refused any alteration in the policy concerning belligerent rights. This apparently mild approach produced a furor of indignation. The Admiralty, discontented with the Government's caution for some time, made no effort to conceal their disappointment. Lord Chatfield wrote that to "carry out our Government's intention, for which there was neither precedent nor law, threw on our Navy a technical task that was exceedingly difficult." [1] He admitted that the Admiralty was pro-Franco, and said that they regarded the denial of belligerent rights to

[1] Chatfield, p. 92.

the Nationalists, after they had command of the sea, as a political trick which sacrificed British interests to those of France. Since the fall of 1936, and throughout 1937, hardly a day passed when the British naval policy in regards to Non-Intervention was not discussed with the Foreign Office. The First Lord of the Admiralty, Sir Samuel Hoare, wrote, "whilst the Board of Admiralty was inclined to Palmerstonian methods, the Foreign Office insisted upon the risks of war." [1] The Government's policy was justified later by international law on the grounds that the customary rules of recognition of belligerency were not applicable because foreign intervention had significantly changed the "civil character" of the war.

Curiously, the Navy, so conservative in tradition, found their views supported not by the Government but by the Labour Opposition. Attlee at the head of an angry party served the Government notice that he would request a day to discuss their failure to give protection to British merchant shipping. And in Commons on April 14th, he charged that the failure to afford protection around Bilbao was surrender of traditional British rights and acquiescence in a serious breach of international law. Provided ships did not carry munitions, their right to trade was undeniable. "General Franco," he said,

promptly sends out by radio a message that any British ship found in Spanish territorial waters will be seized or sunk. That does not seem to have provoked any response from the British Government... There was widespread amazement that this country should step down from the position that it has always taken with regard to the right of vessels at sea.

Sir John Simon, speaking for the Government, replied that if one were to judge the policy fairly, it should be put into the proper setting in regards to Non-Intervention; he strongly denied charges of impartiality and emphasized that the Government already held Franco responsible for any damage suffered by British ships. When Churchill spoke, he tried to impress the Commons with his neutrality. Although a Conservative, he was an outspoken critic of Government policy on practically all major issues *except* Spain. The Non-Intervention Committee, he claimed, in spite of swindlers and cheats, was still a precious thing that kept Britain out of war, and thoughts of breaking the Insurgent blockade would provoke the Germans and Italians into committing further incidents. Even if I were told that Non-Intervention were vitiated by humbug, Churchill said, I would not be daunted. "Hypocrisy, it is said, is the tribute which vice pays to virtue. I am not sure that

[1] Templewood, *Nine Troubled Years*, pp. 255–256.

we can afford to do without any tributes which are going about. I say frankly that I would rather have a peace-keeping hypocrisy than straight forward, brazen vice, taking the form of unlimited war." The *Guardian* described the debate as one of the most spirited, "the air was alive with angry and inarticulate cries, opposition members were shouted down by back benchers." Churchill, finding the House in a mood to be enchanted, being in a "philosophical humor" himself, proceeded to cater to their requirements with phraseology. Eden was not much better; his final speech was mostly a historical lecture about 19th century civil wars and the principle of Non-Intervention.[1] The issue of British naval prestige was more immediate than the war itself and the attempts to subordinate the one to the other seemed to many incongruous.

Bilbao was in a state of siege and starvation might have resulted if merchant shipping had heeded the Government's warnings. For the captains who braved, or appeared to brave, the blockade, there awaited sudden popularity, and enormous profits. Some were given colourful, proletarian names like "Potato" Jones, "Corncob" Jones, or worse still, "Ham and Eggs" Jones. The British were starved for heroes, but romance was short lived. In spite of the Government's admonitions the Nationalist blockade was notoriously ineffective, and after several unsuccessful attempts (foiled in two cases by the British Navy) by Rebel raiders to stop British ships, incidents of molestation became non-existent. The Government's refusal to protect their own shipping under such inglorious circumstances had never before occurred in the memory of most Englishmen. (According to Philip Noel-Baker it was the first time since the defeat of the Armada that Britain had been afraid of a Spanish fleet). The acceptance of threats for facts, the preference to believe anything that strengthened your argument contributed to the political dishonesty of the period. This decision was one of Baldwin's last before retirement.

2. CHAMBERLAIN TAKES OVER

Chamberlain succeeded Baldwin on May 28th, a less than propitious time as events were to show, but Chamberlain seemed equal to any challenge and at once showed himself determined to be more active than his predecessor. Non-Intervention, while still the nominal basis of Spanish policy, would be further diminished. Chamberlain's cabinet

[1] *Guardian*, April 16, 1937.

was just a reshuffle of the old (aside from Hoare's replacement at the Admiralty by Duff Cooper, most of the old faces were back), but there was no question of it being old times; Chamberlain's personality made that impossible. Whereas Baldwin easily delegated authority to subordinates, Chamberlain found it difficult. His relation to men and politics was different, in many respects antithetical. "Baldwin, as Prime Minister, was content to assume that his colleagues were competently discharging their duties, Chamberlain soon showed them that he was not merely chairman in Cabinet, but a general manager who wished to know what his departmental managers were doing, to discuss their problems with them and to keep them up to the work. What is more, he knew his own mind and saw to it that he had his way. An autocrat with all the courage of his convictions, right or wrong," [1] Chamberlain was an advocate of personal diplomacy. In contrast to Baldwin, he did not choose to wait upon events, to have necessity sooner or later dictate a policy; where Baldwin had been leisurily, he would be insistent. If there were to be a policy it would be his policy, and he would set its characteristics. He wanted to come to terms with Hitler, but before he even had a chance to settle in his new office, he was faced with a situation which almost wrecked the Non-Intervention Comittee.

On May 29 the German pocket battleship *Deutschland*, moored in the Balearic island harbour of Iviza, was attacked by Loyalist airplanes. Hitler was furious; the next day, after a conference, he ordered retaliation. Four destroyers proceeded to the Republican port of Almeria, where they bombarded the harbour; the Germans then dispatched a note to the Non-Intervention Committee conveying their intention not to participate in the Committee's deliberations until they were guaranteed against further Republican attacks. Italy followed suit. (Germany had told the Italian Foreign Office that she preferred not to have Italy follow her action in withdrawing from the Non-Intervention Committee. Mussolini, however, contrary to their desire, decided to withdraw from both the London Committee and the naval patrol.) In Berlin Von Neurath informed Sir Nevile Henderson, the British Ambassador, that in the last analysis it was Britain's attitude which influenced the possibility of war. Extremely upset, Henderson kept repeating that Germany should not do the Communists a favour by starting general hostilities. The German Foreign Minister suggested that in view of the situation's gravity Germany expected the British

[1] Amery, p. 225.

Government to "change its previous benevolent attitude toward the Red Rulers in Valencia"; [1] he added that he spent six hours with Hitler in Munich trying to calm him down, but that he had been only partly successful. (Hitler, it seems, went into a rage over the spilling of German blood.)

The Almeria reprisal was regarded by Eden as a case of "national honour," and from his knowledge of the German character, he had the impression that they would now be satisfied. He did not believe that Germany had any intention of precipitating war, but all the same, did everything possible to pacify their feelings; expressing sympathy for the *Deutschland* victims, the British Government accepted the German version of the attack and prevented their retaliation from being discussed in the League. On June 3rd, Britain presented Germany with a proposal upon which she (and Italy) could rejoin the Non-Intervention Committee and the naval patrol. The Spanish Governments were to give their solemn assurance that they would respect foreign ships both on the high seas and in territorial waters and were to designate safety zones in Spanish ports. Britain advised that failure at implementation, resulting in subsequent interference, should result in consultation between the four interested powers to decide further action. (Germany's acceptable revisions demanded that in the event of attack defensive measures be taken immediately before consultation.)

On June 12, a four power agreement was approved, coinciding with German and Italian re-entry to the Non-Intervention Committee. It thus appeared that the Chamberlain Government had passed its first test successfully. During the *Deutschland* affair, Chamberlain thought to make the best of a bad situation by inviting Von Neurath to London to discuss the whole field of Anglo-German relations, but at the Wilhelmstrasse Nevile Henderson was told that any visit to London could only be held after the Foreign Minister's pending trip to the Balkans. On June 6, Henderson repeated the Government's invitation, insisting that the visit would only mean an exchange of views, and not, under any circumstances, formal negotiations. The next day Von Neurath telegraphed from Sofia and proposed the evening of the 23rd as a date he was prepared to go to London. In the same message he instructed the Foreign Ministry to omit from the press communiqué any reference to discussions dealing with the Spanish problem, telling them to inform Henderson that the visit was only possible on the condition that "the question of the guarantee after the Iviza incident has been settled" in

[1] *GD.*, p. 299.

a satisfactory manner.[1] When this was accomplished, nothing seemed to stand in the way of Von Neurath's visit. In this case however Hitler was to be influenced more by men than events. Presently Ambassador to Great Britain, Joachim von Ribbentrop, ambitious and vain, conspired against Neurath's impending visit because he felt it would eclipse his rising star. Fortunately for him Hitler was becoming increasingly suspicious of the Bismarckian tendencies in the Wilhelm-strasse and welcomed those more Nazi in spirit. Ribbentrop probably sensed this change which gave him the courage to openly challenge Foreign Ministry instructions. On June 14 he ignored orders authorizing Germany's return to the Non-Intervention Committee, no doubt justifying his action directly with Hitler.[2] Shortly afterwards Ribbentrop succeeded Neurath as Foreign Minister. The second character in this little policy conspiracy was Mussolini, who apparently feared that Germany in her talks with Britain could be seeking to end the Spanish affair unilaterally. With his own axe to grind, one of the many issues being British recognition of his Ethopian conquest, the Duce suspected Anglo-German conversations might weaken his German alliance, which was an essential factor for strengthening his own position in future negotiations with Britain.[3] Their opposition no doubt was enough to persuade an already suspicious Hitler that conversations with Britain were at the moment inadvisable. A cursory refusal insufficient, it was necessary to find a suitable excuse. The Spanish Civil War gave Hitler unlimited opportunities, and on June 19 the Germans claimed that their cruiser *Leipzig* had been subject to attack by Loyalist submarines. Compounded with doubt of authenticity and lack of verification abroad, there was absence of coordination from within. Radio Stuttgart, for example, broadcasting on the day of the alleged incident, denied that any attack had in fact taken place, and characterized reports to the contrary as malicious fabrications. Germany proceeding anyway demanded the convocation of the four naval powers to which Ribbentrop proposed a joint naval demonstration off Valencia followed by the surrender of all Loyalist submarines. The British and French, rejecting all extreme measures, called for a general inquiry before approving any action. Hitler found this suggestion totally inadmissable.

In Berlin on the same day the "attack" was announced, Henderson

---

[1] *Ibid.*, p. 313.
[2] *GD.*, p. 333.
[3] *Ibid.*, pp. 338–340.

received a letter from Neurath cancelling the London visit. On the 20th, a Sunday, Henderson tried to speak with the Foreign Minister but found him impossible to locate until late that evening. Henderson argued that the *Leipzig* incident made Neurath's presence in London all the more desirable and said that he could not accept his refusal as definite until he had the opportunity to speak directly with Hitler. The interview took place the next day; Hitler, having just returned from the funeral of the *Deutschland* victims, was so emotional and tractable that Henderson was at a loss for explanations.[1] Hitler so sharply rebuked Chamberlain's overtures that he was left without any tangible leads for the future. Chamberlain had used the *Deutschland* affair as an excuse to invite Neurath, but Hitler had used the *Leipzig* affair as an excuse to sabotage this visit. The game could be played both ways and the moral was obvious: to mix Spanish affairs with other problems was more dangerous than rewarding; it was therefore best to ignore Spanish problems as much as possible. (It was this interpretation which provoked the major disagreement between Chamberlain and his Foreign Secretary, who always insisted that agreement on Spain constitute the center of any rapprochement.)

On June 23, with progress in the Four Power Conference still at zero, the Germans announced, their minimum demands having been rejected, they once more had regained their freedom of action, and, as a first step, would withdraw from the Naval Patrol. The British immediately became concerned about Germany's intentions toward Non-Intervention, but Neurath assured them that Germany was not interested in further complicating the situation. (Withdrawal from control did not mean Germany was willing to remove her ships from Spanish waters; quite the contrary, for Germany, in a series of secret fleet movements, reinforced her flotilla in the area. Italy, out of the patrol, also made no moves to return ships to home waters and newspapers reported that Italy was again sending troops.) The gap in the patrol scheme created one simultaneously in British policy. Britain had hoped the next step would be withdrawal of troops. A stronger line was implied; on June 21, in the Non-Intervention Sub-Committee Lord Plymouth hinted that Britain might consider revision of her policy if more fruitful results were not forthcoming. Eden tended to look for the silver lining; in spite of German (and Italian) refusals to participate in control, he found comfort that there had been no further reprisals and that Germany and Italy had not withdrawn from Non-Inter-

[1] Henderson, pp. 67–69.

vention. In a conversation with the American Ambassador on June 25 he expressed his regret that Neurath's visit had been cancelled, but added that since the German Foreign Minister had a restraining influence on Hitler it was probably just as well that he did not leave Berlin at this time; Eden said that he had tried to reassure Delbos, who had called him up greatly disturbed in the middle of the night, that the situation, although serious, was not as grave as it appeared.[1] France was in no mood to tolerate a reversal on control efforts. With vast quantities of supplies, especially Italian reinforcements, anticipated, it was obvious that should Hitler and Mussolini establish a hostile Fascist state in Spain, France would be placed in an extremely dangerous position. Camille Chautemps (French Premier since June 22) viewed the situation pessimistically: "all his information from London indicated that Chamberlain was still inclined to adopt a policy of "wait and see" coupled with a policy of attempting to detach Germany from Italy." He realized that any policy France might have required British support, which he was sceptical of getting.[2]

On June 29, Britain and France proposed a joint plan whereby they would themselves fill the gap in the patrol scheme. Germany and Italy objected. Counter proposals were submitted including the clearly unacceptable recognition of belligerent rights. Further deadlock. Most likely to shock Britain out of her lethargy, France made it known that unless the effectiveness of the control scheme were soon restored to the efficiency level prior to the *Deutschland* incident, she would no longer consider herself bound by Non-Intervention and would open the Franco-Spanish frontier.[3] The meeting of the Non-Intervention Committee scheduled for July 9th, gave France little hope any compromise measures would succeed, but she was willing to use it to encourage British action. According to Léger, the French Government, attempting to make Britain realize her "responsibilities," wanted to use the clear-cut majority of the Non-Intervention Committee for support of Britain and France in the imposition of control. Léger was confident that if Britain and France should now take a strong position, Germany and Italy would back down.[4] A get-tough policy, however, was contrary to both British practice and intention, as Léger himself realized; the ensuing events proceeded along the lines he had generally predicted.

[1] *USD.*, 1937, I, p. 342.
[2] *Ibid.*, pp. 347–348.
[3] *Guardian*, July 9, 1937. Her motives were also in the nature of self-defense. See *USD.*, 1937, I, p. 347.
[4] *USD.*, 1937, I, pp. 356–357.

At the Committee session Italian conduct (they accused the British Government of being a principal source of aid to the Loyalists) seemed calculated to wreck the Committee. But before this hopeless situation could become desperate the Dutch delegate proposed that Britain make an additional effort to work for a solution, and consequently a new plan, quickly thrown together by Eden, was ready by July 15 and accepted forthwith as a basis for discussion. The British proposal submitted on July 14 became a source of inspiration for all those which followed. It was divided into five sections: reconstruction of the system of supervision; means for making supervision more effective; withdrawal of foreign nationals; priority of execution; immediate steps authorized by the British Government. However, significance lay less in the content of the proposal itself than in the opening statement, for unless accepted in the spirit of compromise, "unless a greater spirit of international cooperation is evident than has been achieved in the past, this scheme will fail, and the nations of Europe will be faced with a new and infinitely more dangerous situation." [1] The naval patrol, according to the new scheme, would be replaced by a system of international patrol officers, stationed in Spanish ports; furthermore, it was suggested that restricted belligerent rights might be accorded to the Spanish Governments, when a plan for withdrawing foreign nationals was working with success. Eden's characterization carried little conviction, but the plan, essentially compromise, represented a fair balance between the various points of view and probably constituted the best practical arrangement that could be found under the circumstances. The Quai d'Orsay gave them practically no chance of success. At a lunch with the American and British Ambassadors Delbos, highly critical at the way this situation had been handled, was openly displeased that France had not been consulted. He told Sir Eric Phipps, much to the latter's embarrassment, that the British Government by her action "had withdrawn from co-operation in the Spanish affair and had placed itself midway between France on the one hand and Germany on the other hand." So obvious a move would only encourage the dictators.[2] In the latest British proposal the inclusion of belligerent rights, despite consistent French opposition, without prior consultation, added to French discomfort. France took comfort that the withdrawal scheme had little chance of success, emphazing in the Sub-Committee there be no discussion of belligerent rights until the resolution of volunteer withdrawal.

[1] *Cmd.* 5521.
[2] *USD.*, 1937, I, pp. 360–361.

Disregard of France had been fairly frequent in the past but under Chamberlain it seemed more obvious and intentional. The prejudice engendered by the innumerable cabinet crises of the Third Republic on the mind of that Englishman, traditionally accustomed to government stability, resulted in his unfortunate downgrading of French advice. There was little excuse for this. During the Spanish Civil War the French Foreign Office was one of the most stable ministries; not only did Yvon Delbos remain as Foreign Minister through almost the entire period, but natural equilibrium at the Quai d'Orsay existed through the Civil Service, headed by the lucid, well-informed Alexis Léger. The French were put into an extremely difficult position, not at all appreciated by Chamberlain, who trying to negotiate with Germany and Italy, expected at the same time France, although not a participant herself, to approve and support all British leads. Chamberlain held that nothing should stand in the way of negotiations with Germany and Italy; he disregarded the Non-Intervention Committee, and on one occasion admitted that "it was rather difficult for him to follow in detail the complicated and abstruse formulae which emerged one after another from the hairsplitting debates." [1]

In the Sub-Committee the Germans and Italians insisted on having recognition of belligerency *before* discussion of withdrawals. Italy proved the most intransigent, but in a bitter attack she charged it was Moscow's dogmatic insistence on prior withdrawal which was deadlocking the Committee. Russia indeed did prove stubborn, but Italy had already raised enough objections and reservations to ruin any discussion. It is difficult to assess Russian motives, but her action gave Germany and Italy the opportunity to detract from their own culpability (also France was probably saved a showdown with Britain on the belligerent rights issue, if Britain chose later to ignore the priority of withdrawals) and led to her further isolation. In any case, it is important to note that the Committee became deadlocked on a secondary issue before arriving at the more important question of controls. Why this was so, was partly the fault of Britain. Of course, one could argue with reason that Italy or Germany would have torpedoed the talks anyway, but this still does not change the fact that Eden, in trying to steer a middle course, enabled attention to be diverted from the meeting's principal purpose. Britain tried to resolve the deadlock by use of normal diplomatic channels but they came to nothing; she then tried another tactic. Hoping at least to have some progress on a

[1] Told to Ciano, *Diplomatic Papers*, p. 179.

lesser issue, the fate of the naval patrol scheme, she proposed (on August 6) that a commission be established to report on means of "restoring and improving" naval observation around Spanish coasts. However, before recommendations could be made attention was distracted by attacks on merchant shipping in the Mediterranean.

3. THE BOULEVARD DES INCONNUS

A year's adventure in Spain gave Mussolini many vexations. He might have had the general support of his party (as well as the Vatican) but among his people the war was increasingly unpopular. In Spain troop morale was extremely low; after the rout of Guadalajara the difficulty in persuading engagement in even minor offensive action had delayed victory over the Basques, slowed the offensive against Santander, and strained relations with Franco. In addition, while France considered opening their Spanish frontier, Russia continued to send aid. But Mussolini still had confidence in the attitude of Great Britain. There was cause to believe that she did not desire a Republican victory, and was more concerned with events after than during the war. Mussolini, however, was not fool enough to deliberately wish her estrangement, and thus he promoted better relations, while concurrently planning bolder action.

The Duce had written Chamberlain a personal letter expressing his desire for Anglo-Italian friendship, which he had entrusted to Count Dino Grandi, the Italian Ambassador in London, with the instructions that Grandi use it only "when he thought that the moment was propitious." [1] On July 19 Eden gave a speech in the Commons which made such an excellent impression, that Grandi, encouraged to give Chamberlain Mussolini's message,[2] told Eden on July 24 that he would like to see the Prime Minister. Chamberlian first thought that Mussolini was simply going to protest his good intentions claiming "no designs in the Mediterranean, nor on Spanish territory," but he planned to see Grandi anyway "to find out whether there is any nigger in this woodpile." [3] Chamberlain saw Grandi twice on July 27, at which time he

---

[1] Chamberlain's phrase, 21 February 1938, in the Commons.
[2] Eden had said "free traffic through and out of the Mediterranean is the common interest of Great Britain and of all the Mediterranean Powers" and we wish to live in peace and friendship with our neighbours in the Mediterranean as elsewhere, for "while we will defend our own we covet nought of theirs."
[3] Feiling, p. 330.

handed the Ambassador a letter of his own. The Prime Minister later wrote, "I did not show my letter to the Foreign Secretary, for I had the feeling that he would object to it." [1] Mussolini again wrote, at the same time terminating, as a goodwill gesture, a press boycott of English news. The *Times* called the exchange "a turning point in Anglo-Italian relations"; [2] Ciano said it was a "great stride forward," remarking that "the difficulties in recent months in the way of mutual understanding have been decidedly psychological rather than concrete." [3] The British Foreign Office though, much to Chamberlain's annoyance, continued to regard Mussolini as a sort of Machiavelli.

* * *

Heretofore attacks against shipping had been mostly confined to Spanish vessels in Spanish waters; however, during the month of August, after a period of relative calm, the situation changed. Mussolini's intervention took on a new dimension and what had originally been an intention to stop Russian transports became completely indiscriminate; not only were ships of all nationalities [4] attacked, but Spanish territorial waters meant anywhere in the Mediterranean. In addition to the submarines which he himself employed, Mussolini encouraged Franco to use warships and planes; as a result during the first week and a half at least ten ships were assailed. Italy immediately denied any complicity, blaming the Soviets. Britain made no accusations, but there were few doubts of the originator. In Paris the *Boulevard des Italiens* was dubbed the *Boulevard des Inconnus*. Ciano unrealistically hoped that recent troubles in the Far East would divert British attention. But the British Admiralty clamoured for action and immediately took defensive measures. On August 6, the destroyer *Gallant* replied to an attack with an anti-aircraft barrage and later two destroyers warned four Spanish warships that they were prepared to defend a threatened freighter. On the 17th, the Government authorized the Admiralty not only to defend, but counterattack any submarine which tried to attack British shipping. But as an attack against a British steamer revealed, even this was insufficient; therefore, on August 25, Britain reinforced her Mediterranean flotilla. At the same time she

[1] *Ibid.*
[2] *Times*, August 3, 1937.
[3] *Ibid.*, August 7, 1937.
[4] i.e. British, French, Danish, Greek, Spanish, Russian, Panamanian and Italian (the last evidentally by mistake).

protested to Franco that future attacks would not be tolerated. Chamberlain hoped this action would not endanger future Italian negotiations proposed for September, and despite contrary evidence,[1] was very careful not to label Italy guilty. On August 15, in Rome, the British *Chargé d'Affaires*, Ingram, told Ciano of British concern but took special pains to emphasize that this did not constitute a protest, but was merely a wish that relations "should not be troubled by unforeseeable and deplorable complications." [2] Ciano was condescendingly evasive; he denied any Italian connection, reiterating that the attacks were perpetrated by Russia. Ingram seemed convinced and Ciano was pleased. Four days later Ingram stressed his Government's intention to negotiate, but asked a delay, giving as a reason the death of Sir Eric Drummond's brother. At the same time he mentioned that Italian airplanes were carrying out observations on British ships. Ciano quickly answered that these observations were part of normal reconnaisance. Ingram's satisfaction conveyed a weak and impotent attitude which undermined Britain's position with Mussolini who regarded Chamberlain's efforts to eliminate misunderstandings as a sign of weakness.

On September 25 Santander fell to the Rebels. Mussolini elatedly told Ciano that he would now make the defeatists of Guadalajara regret their pessimism. Dropping all pretense of Non-Intervention, he exchanged telegrams with General Franco in which he spoke of the valiant contribution his troops made to victory and their comradeship of arms. The victory parade was celebrated in true antique style. The Italian division entered the defeated city in triumph; in front, their general on a chestnut mount, next came the Spanish cavalry which was followed, classically enough, by a column of prisoners. Ciano ordered the Basque canons and flags sent to Rome and in high spirits commanded a night bombardment of Valencia. One must size the right opportunity to terrorize the enemy, he concluded.[3] Shipping attacks, quiescent for two weeks, now began with renewed force. Clearly Britain would have to take other steps if she ever wanted peace in the Mediterranean.

By the end of August Britain and France were discussing both the question of attack and the entire future of Non-Intervention. Mussolini's telegram to Franco had convinced Chautemps that a continuation

[1] The Admiralty was able to intercept and decodify transmissions from Italian submarines in the Mediterranean. See *GD.*, p. 443, and *USD.*, 1937, I, p. 394.
[2] *Ciano's Diplomatic Papers*, p. 134.
[3] Ciano, *Journal Politique*, p. 19.

of the work of the Comittee would be impossible; however, he "saw no alternative program which would not involve most serious consequences." [1] He (and also Léger) thought present circumstances made it extremely difficult for Britain to continue her policy of reconciliation with Mussolini. Chamberlain reluctantly came to the same conclusion. "Unfortunately," he later stated, "certain incidents took place in the Mediterranean which, in our opinion, rendered it impossible that conversations at that time could have any chance of success." [2] On September 2nd, therefore, Britain accepted the French suggestion for a special Mediterranean conference, taking place outside the Non-Intervention Committee. Britain's decision was no doubt hastened by an attack the previous night on H.M.S. *Havoc* followed the next morning, during an emergency meeting at the Foreign Office, by the sinking of the British tanker *Woodford*. That afternoon it was held necessary to further strengthen British naval forces.

The Government's anxiety to begin the conference as soon as possible pleased the French. (Mussolini, though, was not worried for he did not believe Britain wanted a showdown.) The next few days Britain and France discussed arrangements. Geneva was at first suggested as a possible location but, not wanting to antagonize Germany and Italy who were estranged from the League of Nations, a town nearby was chosen. After some dispute, ten countries were invited; [3] and communiqués, emphasizing the need for haste, proposed September 10 as the date of convocation. Above all, Britain desired the participation of Germany and Italy and therefore made it plain that this conference would only be concerned with the specific question of attacks against shipping; all other questions would be handled by the Non-Intervention Committee. Russia did not want Italy at the Conference; fearing that the Conference would produce a four power pact to her disadvantage (she was already isolated in the Non-Intervention Committee), and also acting out of national pride for the damage suffered to her ships, she hoped to insure Italian non-participation by accusing Italy of the sinkings and demanding compensation.[4] The plan worked. Upon receipt of the Russian note Italy informed Germany that this development had created a new situation, and that the invitation,

---

[1] *USD.*, 1937, I, p. 381.
[2] In the Commons, 21 February 1938.
[3] Roughly divided into two groups: 1) Mediterranean – Albania, Egypt, Turkey, Greece, Italy, Yugoslavia; 2) Black Sea – Bulgaria, Rumania, U.S.S.R.; plus Britain, France and Germany.
[4] *GD.*, pp. 440–443; Fisher, pp. 445–447; *Survey*, 1937, II, pp. 345–346.

hitherto looked upon not unfavourably, would now have to be studied
further. The Russian action was a bluff. There had been newspaper
reports that Russian sailors had been able to take photographs of
Italian submarines, but this was not true. Litvinov had correctly
reasoned that Italy would not demand evidence. On September 9, after
mutual consultation, the Italians and Germans, in view of the Russian
accusations, declined any part in the conference; they recommended
that instead of bothering with a special conference, the Non-Intervention Committee should be authorized to handle the matter.
Knowing the history of the London Committee this suggestion, taken
as a desire to destroy the conference, was refused.

4 THE MEDITERRANEAN CONFERENCE

Touristically, the village of Nyon has many advantages: situated on
Lake Geneva, dominated by a sixteenth century chateau, the quays
are lined with spider-like plane trees and, assuming clear weather, the
view extends across the Lake to the French Alps. As the place to hold
a conference, though, it left much to be desired. Ill equipped for anything larger than local gatherings of farmers, the hotel accommodations
were inadequate, the telephone facilities worse. Most of the delegates
preferred to stay in Geneva 14 miles away and commute. The *Salle
Communale*, attractively enough provisioned with gladioli and chry-
santhemums, was a huge barn almost devoid of Committee rooms,
"part theatre, part concert hall, part village meeting place." But
technical inconveniences were not all; the weather was horrible: rain,
falling temperatures and gusty wind. Fortunately, the conference
lasted only a few days.

The British arrived, their portfolios bulging with already formulated
plans. The previous evening Eden, Vansittart and Chatfield had dinner
with Chautemps and Delbos at the Quai d'Orsay where they reached
complete agreement on the proposals to the forthcoming conference.
Thus when the Nyon Conference officially opened the afternoon of
September 10 everything had been prepared to expedite the deliberations. Upon Eden's nomination Delbos was unanimously elected
president. In a short opening speech the French Foreign Minister
outlined what he considered the purpose of the Conference, the cor-
rection of an intolerable situation by reinforcing the rule of international law towards shipping in the Mediterranean. He expressed his

regret that Germany and Italy should "have thought it their duty to decline the invitation sent to them and should have added that in their view the problem could be delt with in another fashion"; only by treating the problem as "definite in itself," and not part of the problems of the Non-Intervention Committee, could a speedy settlement be had.[1] Delbos was followed by Litvinov who showed himself a great deal more polemical. "His speech," said the *Times*, "bore the evidence of eleventh-hour revision." Although not mentioning Italy by name, he made it clear who was responsible for this "state piracy," saying that Russia, while not encouraged by recent events to trust the actions of other states, would nevertheless try cooperating with any international effort to solve the problem. Eden then took the floor and, emphasizing his regret that Germany and Italy were not present, said that the Conference would no doubt keep them informed of the transactions in the hope that they later adhere to the agreed provisions. The Conference formed a standing committee which went into private session.

At this meeting the Anglo-French technical plan was immediately accepted as the basis for discussion. Under its terms the Mediterranean west of Malta would be patrolled by Britain and France while the eastern remainder, a part of which being offered to Italy, would be parcelled out among the other participants,[2] including Russia; Germany was not included. This plan was opposed by the smaller powers, who, feeling they had inadequate destroyer force to participate and unwilling to assume risks which might involve them seriously with a stronger power, preferred participation only in name. Italy it was believed had also objected, telling Britain "that she could not allow the establishment in the Mediterranean" of this system.[3] Britain therefore changed the original draft and by the next meeting a revised agreement was ready for the delegates' further consideration. This scheme, adopted two days later, made the naval patrol essentially the responsibility of Great Britain and France. Litvinov considered the resolutions too mild, wanting a definite agreement that any submarine engaging in acts of piracy would be sunk; he considered the agreement equivalent to recognition of belligerency. He received no support from either Eden or Delbos. "The agreement," wrote the American Consul in Geneva, "is considered here as a severe defeat for Russia and it is

---

[1] *Times*, September 11, 1937.
[2] i.e. Bulgaria, Egypt, Greece, Roumania, Turkey and Yugoslavia.
[3] *USD.*, 1937, I, p. 398.

believed that Russia will now join with Spain in strongly pushing their cases against Italy in the League." [1] With Russian objections ignored, the other proposals were easily handled. Lord Chatfield was pleased that, aside from England and France, nobody knew anything about submarines.[2] The agreement had been completed in the remarkable time of two days; it was signed on the 14th and took effect that midnight. The principal sea routes and the area of the Western Mediterranean being patrolled by Great Britain and France meant a sizable increase of their Mediterranean destroyer fleet, the bulk of which was British. The patrolling ships were authorized to attack any submarine which struck a non-Spanish merchantman and in fact any submarine in the area where such an attack had occurred. (Later these instructions included any submarine submerged in patrol areas.) To facilitate execution, ships were advised to follow certain agreed upon and defined routes.

Acting on a long time practice that it is best to reform an adversary by putting him in a position of responsibility, Britain worked for the inclusion of Italy. Eden's suggestion at the beginning of the Conference that Italy be kept informed of all the proceedings was approved by the standing committee without discussion; in fact, throughout the talks it was assumed "that Italy would participate in the patrol." [3] Italy, however, was hardly grateful. The Italian Ambassador in Spain said that the Nyon Conference agreement would be discriminatory against Franco. Mussolini apparently realizing that Italy's presence or absence in the scheme would make little difference, made plans to join, though considering the naval patrol as originally offered prejudicial to Italian prestige. Germany, not interested in joining, let Italy take any leads she deemed necessary. Knowing the Italian reluctance to associate in any inferior capacity, Eden, in presenting Ciano with the text of the supplementary agreement,[4] on September 18,[5] took special care to be solicitous. Ciano, informed several days before that Eden and Delbos were ready to talk terms, was determined to let them make the first move,[6] and when Britain and France showed

[1] *Ibid.*
[2] Chatfield, p. 93.
[3] *USD.*, 1937, I, p. 396.
[4] Signed in Geneva on the 17th, it extended the original Nyon declaration to include attacks by aircraft and warships. *Cmd.* 5569.
[5] On the same day it was decided to discontinue the naval patrol effective the previous April. In view of the fact that Germany and Italy had withdrawn it would have been too difficult for Britain and France to carry this commitment and Nyon too. It was hoped that by increased vigilance of land observers obligations could be maintained.
[6] Ciano, *Journal Politique*, p. 30.

willingness to grant Italy equality, he was overjoyed, considering their *démarche* an offer to modify the Nyon Agreement according to Italian desires. It was a great joke that Italy should pass from a position of marauders of the Mediterranean to that of policemen, while Russia was excluded from control. Britain who had never considered the Italian demand for equality as offering serious complications, since there never had existed any question about it not being granted, regarded Italian boasts of diplomatic victory with amusement. Mussolini had been tamed not by persuasion or concession, but by Anglo-French action, which made him realize that he had gone too far. In any case, there was no question that Mussolini was not interested in creating a favourable impression. On September 21 Italy agreed to participate in a special technical conference on arrangements to include Italy in the Nyon Agreement. At the same time Ciano told the British *Chargé d'Affaires* that "there was no present intention of permitting the dispatch of further volunteers to Spain." [1] The next day in Geneva Mussolini's representative, Bova-Scoppa, in talks with Delbos, emphasized that Italy "had no intention of making the smallest change in the territorial status of Spain; that she had no designs upon the Balearic Islands, and that the integrity of the continental and insular territory of Spain would be strictly respected." [2] These conversations were characterized in certain newspapers as negotiations of high policy. They are better understood as an attempt by Mussolini to better his position at the forthcoming Paris talks or as a desire to appear conciliatory before his visit to Germany. A German report said that the Italian representative had received instructions from Rome "to counteract once more the rumors concerning Italy's alleged territorial aspirations in Spain spread by the French in Geneva on the occasion of the present Mediterranean negotiations in Paris." [3] It was reported elsewhere that Delbos significantly assured Bova-Scoppa that the claims of Italy to parity would receive "sympathetic consideration" at the Paris talks. [4]

Profiting from this atmosphere, the naval talks, which began September 27, progressed rapidly and harmoniously; unattended by foreign office or embassy personnel, the naval experts were able to handle minor differences (chiefly concerning zonal delimitation) with more technical than political dispatch. Britain was pleased at the Italian willingness to cooperate. Under the terms of the agreement signed

[1] *Cmd.* 5570.
[2] *Ibid.*
[3] *GD.*, p. 455.
[4] *Survey*, 1937, II, p. 352.

September 30, Italy was assigned a patrol area in the Adriatic and Tyrrhenian seas; and until such date (November 11) as Italian participation became effective, the patrol would be assumed by Britain and France.

The Nyon Conference on the whole seemed rather routine. There were no secret protocols, and nothing occurred that had not generally been predicted; the Conference's only casualty was Lord Chatfield who ate so much rich food at the opening banquet that he was out of action for two days. Its results however were noticeable. Submarine and other attacks fell by about seventy percent; almost totally at first but the following spring they resumed somewhat. In general Nyon satisfactorily solved a problem which arose because there was a war in Spain; it made no attempt to solve the war itself. Léger wanted to transfer the momentum gained by Nyon to the problem of preventing further Italian troop movements; but while he thought Eden would be in favour, he rightly guessed Chamberlain's hostility. Scrupulously divorced from the rest of the war, the Nyon Conference set limits on Mussolini's Spanish policy. The Conference was primarily the achievement of Anthony Eden and, while Chamberlain was not disappointed with the results, he nevertheless could not forget that Nyon's great success came at the "expense of Anglo-Italian relations." The Italians, he wrote in his diary "made the Russian note a pretext for abstention as the Russians meant they should, and now with intense chagrin they see collaboration between the British and French fleets, of a kind never known before... It would be amusing, if it were not also dangerous."[1] Eden's own evaluation concentrated on the role exercised by British and French cooperation. "Nyon," he wrote, "has much increased our authority among the nations, at a time when we needed such an increase badly." [2] Eden implied that the decisive part played by this co-partnership might well be extended to other aspects of the Civil War.

Chamberlain was not discouraged. Italy's apparent willingness to participate in the naval patrol was, at least superficially, promising; and the Bova-Scoppa talks had suggested that tri-partite discussions were necessary to solve the problem of foreign intervention. Chamberlain did not believe, as Churchill,[3] that Mussolini only understood superior force, and that the advantages gained by Nyon could only be secured with a show of strength. The *Guardian* sensed insincerity among

---

[1] Feiling, p. 331.
[2] Churchill, pp. 192–193.
[3] *Ibid.*

those who defended Italian adhesion to Nyon in the "hope that if the Nyon pill is sweetened... she will suddenly see the light, undergo conversion, and withdraw from Spain." [1] From the Government's point of view this was beside the point. According to Lord Halifax, Britain would "try to secure that the issue of the Spanish Civil War should not be permitted materially to offset the relations of the Mediterranean Powers and their position in the Mediterranean." [2] Nyon was clearly directed towards this end.

Even if feeble application of Non-Intervention meant the end of a *genuine* Spanish democracy, there was no obligation that Britain run the risks of war, but towards Italy this policy was self-defeating, for to have success with Mussolini Britain had to challenge his Spanish adventure. It was all right to talk, as Churchill did, about transforming the Mediterranean naval position to protect the British Empire from Italian threats, but, to allow Mussolini continual *carte blanche* in Spain meant an ultimate defeat of purpose. If Britain backed down because not to do so might mean war, then she could not expect to proceed beyond the barest containment of the war and the prospect of bringing Mussolini to his senses would remain a vain hope. The possibility of sidetracking the war only had validity if there existed complete willingness to resign success in other remotely connected areas.

[1] *Guardian*, October 1, 1937.
[2] In the Lords, 21 October 1937.

CHAPTER V

THEMES AND VARIATIONS

I. GENEVA DEBATES

From the December Council meeting,[1] it was not until May 1937 that the League again considered the Spanish Civil War in any detail. On May 19, following several previous protests, Spain made a formal request to have the Council include a discussion of Spain on its agenda. (At the Council meeting in December Spain had reserved the right to raise the question later when they saw fit.) The first meeting of the 97th Council opened May 24. Four days later the Loyalist delegate, Alvarez Del Vayo, submitted a collection of documents known as the *White Paper*, showing without doubt that there were complete units of the Italian army, acting in their zone of "occupation" as if Spain were a conquered country.[2] Alvarez Del Vayo denounced the control scheme as a failure and claimed that if "the League is to have a future, the struggle in Spain cannot end without the League adopting a clear and firm position.[3] As before, although not expecting her demands to be fulfilled, Spain hoped to create a favourable public opinion, especially in Great Britain, which would demand the strengthening of Non-Intervention.

Since the Council's December meeting, British League policy had undergone no revision; even her tactics of distracting attention from League affairs by other diplomatic moves remained the same. Making approaches in various European capitals, Britain proposed plans of armistice and schemes of withdrawal. The *démarches* were given wide coverage in the European press. An American diplomatic report regarded these British moves as "largely an effort to dissociate them-

[1] Chapter II, part 3.
[2] These documents, comprising letters, orders, records, etc., captured at the battle of Guadalajara were published in the *Official Journal* as special supplement no. 165.
[3] *Official Journal*, Council, 1937, p. 320.

selves in advance from the Spanish presentation of their case to the Council and perhaps by some means sidetrack action or at least to minimize the political and popular effects of what may transpire." [1] Britain, with the help of France, also used direct pressure. On a visit to Paris a few weeks before, Alvarez Del Vayo had been cautioned at the Quai D'Orsay to be moderate in the presentation of the *White Paper*,[2] and, immediately upon arrival in Geneva, he was buttonholed by Eden and Delbos. Eden at first wanted complete suppression of all the Spanish evidence, but finally agreed that French and British support would depend on the way Alvarez Del Vayo presented his case. Britain concentrated next on the press. One journalist recalled "at the press reception on 27 May 1937, the British correspondents were told by the representative of the Foreign Office that the Secretary of State (Mr. Eden) hoped that they would write as little as possible about the "White Paper" in their papers. The representative of the Foreign Office pointed out that the publication of long extracts from the *White Book* or a long summary would be most distasteful to Signor Mussolini and might make him more difficult to deal with in the negotiations that were going to begin about the withdrawal of non-Spanish combatants from Spain." [3] During the meeting itself, (May 28) Eden, on one occasion in a state of tension, left his place on the Council stand and, sitting down next to New Zealand's representative William Jordan, proceeded in full view of everybody to edit the other's speech.[4] When Eden spoke he tried to refer the Spanish question back to the London Committee. Talking about progress in the enforcement of Non-Intervention and steps currently taken for the withdrawal of "volunteers," he vaguely expressed hope in arriving at some tangible agreement. The United Kingdom, he remarked, was after all "only one of the twenty-seven governments represented on the London Committee" and had "no special responsibility for the work done." At the end of his speech Eden stressed the British Government's two prime objectives: "First, to do the utmost which lay in its power to ensure that the Spanish conflict should not spread and involve all Europe in its consequences. Secondly, to ensure that whatever the final outcome of the Spanish Civil War, the territorial integrity of Spain should be preserved." [5] Britain's opportunity to exercise influence was facilitated

---

[1] *USD.*, 1937, I, pp. 301–302.
[2] *Ibid.*, pp. 300–301.
[3] Dell, p. 152; see also *Guardian*, May 31, 1937.
[4] *New Statesman*, June 12, 1937, p. 953.
[5] *Journal Official*, Council, 1937, pp. 323–324.

by the position given Spanish questions on the agenda. Apparently the League had the tendency to leave subjects which could be pre-decided last, for in this way more time was created for behind the scene maneuvring. During the Civil War, Spanish affairs were invariably put last; it would be too disingenuous to say that this was coincidence.

The final resolution produced May 29 was the result of private Anglo-Spanish negotiations and several secret meetings. Alvarez Del Vayo had wanted definite dates set for the withdrawal of volunteers and also a statement proclaiming Spain's right to control her own destiny, (i.e. her right to buy arms). Against British veto it was impossible to gain their inclusion. As a result the final draft was a general confirmation of principles of territorial integrity and political independence and was little different from the one made in December; it condemned violation of international law and praised efforts expended to make the war more humane.

* * *

On August 21, 1937, the Republic again appealed to the League, demanding under the terms of Article 11 that the Council examine the situation in the Mediterranean. In the meantime the Nyon Conference had however fairly well decided the matter and by September 16 many of Spain's arguments were irrelevant, leaving the Spanish delegate, Juan Negrin, (head of the Spanish Government) only opportunity to criticize the Conference itself. Deprecating Spain's exclusion from Nyon, Negrin strongly attacked the failure to apply the Agreement to Spanish as well as foreign shipping; he demanded Italy be named the aggressor. The resolution produced on October 5, couched in generalities like so many others, overlooked Spain's objections, noted the effectiveness of Nyon, and deplored violations to humanity and international law.

At the sessions of the 18th League Assembly which met from September 18 to October 2, in what constituted the climax of her efforts before the League, the Republic tried to force a resolution directly ending Non-Intervention. Alvarez Del Vayo called it Spain's attempt "to give the British and French governments an opportunity of bringing their influence to bear on Berlin and Rome, in order to enforce the withdrawal of non-Spanish combatants.[1] There was little doubt that sympathy was in Spain's favour; "the ambiance of the

[1] *Freedom's Battle*, p. 42.

League itself was preponderately on the Republican side"; [1] intensified by the incidents of Guernica and Almeria their sympathy was stronger than before, but it was coupled with despair.

The *Times* correspondent sensed throughout the whole discussion a feeling of retribution for past weakness; [2] a gloom, intensified by the weather, hung over all the deliberations, "rain fell, day after day, torrential, clammy, cold. Within the overheated rooms of the League buildings, delegates, secretaries and journalists freely bestowed influenza upon each other." [3] Reflected in the character of the general debate was the desire to avoid mention of the war as much as possible, while doubts as to whether Non-Intervention could continue were not replaced by suggestions offering any alternative. Negrin tried to shock Britain and France into action; he reminded them of the Italian position in the Balearics, the long-range guns aimed at Gibraltar, the threats to Southern France. Eden though remained satisfied that the Non-Intervention policy was serving its purpose in preventing a European conflict. France was more affected. (In Paris it was commonly held that unless a great improvement were shown in the enforcement of Non-Intervention the Spanish frontiers would be opened. At the signature of the Nyon supplementary agreement, September 17, France had agreed to postpone such a decision for "a further limited period.") [4] During the debates Yvon Delbos was clear that his country had less patience with Non-Intervention violations than Britain. On the 20th of September, the Spanish Question was referred to the Political Committee, where during the next week a special Committee tried to formulate a resolution. The British and French delegates opposed their Spanish and Russian colleagues in a series of bitter exchanges. The Spanish position had been outlined in the General League Debate by Negrin who demanded,

(1) That the aggression of Germany and Italy in Spain be recognized as such.
(2) That, in consequence of this recognition, the League examine as rapidly as possible the means by which that aggression may be brought to an end.
(3) That full rights once more be given to the Spanish Government to freely acquire all the war material it may consider necessary.
(4) That the non-Spanish combatants be withdrawn from Spanish territory.
(5) That the measures to be adopted for security in the Mediterranean be extended to Spain, and that Spain be granted her legitimate share in them.[5]

[1] Walters, p. 705.
[2] *Times*, September 20, 1937.
[3] Freda White, *Geneva*, 1937 (pamphlet).
[4] *Survey*, 1937, II, pp. 357–358.
[5] *Official Journal*, 18th Assembly, p. 54.

It was on these points that Del Vayo now insisted. The Spaniard viewed the session as a personal struggle between himself and the British delegate, Walter Elliot, whose counter-proposals ignored what he considered fundamental. Alvarez Del Vayo pressed for concrete assurances, repeatedly insisting on time limits for withdrawal of foreign troops. Elliot finally conceded that if German and Italian troops had not been withdrawn in the near future Britain would reverse her thinking on Non-Intervention. Alvarez Del Vayo then insisted on a precise definition of the words "near future"; he was ambiguously told "probably an earlier date than the Spanish delegate thinks." [1] Under British and French pressure, (specifically under the insistence of Léon Blum who told Del Vayo that to insist upon naming Germany and Italy as aggressors and the freedom to purchase munitions might prejudice the impending Anglo-French conversations with Italy),[2] Del Vayo was forced to forego most of his original points.

When the Drafting Committee referred the resolution back to the Political Committee, it was covered with reservations. There was general agreement on the usual clauses; non-interference in internal affairs of other states, obligations to respect territorial integrity, etc., but translation into practice became another matter. Albania and Portugal insisted that the phrase "veritable foreign army corps on Spanish soil, which represents foreign intervention" be changed to read "veritable armed forces on both sides on Spanish soil," and in the section calling for the end of Non-Intervention if effectively impossible, the phrase "members of the League which are parties to the Non-Intervention agreement will consider ending the policy" should be qualified with the word "certain" inserted before "members," the verb "consider" modified with "might." [3] These amendments were over-ruled. The final resolution, without mentioning countries specifically, made reference to diplomatic action taken by Britain and France, hoped that their efforts would be successful in securing the immediate withdrawal of the foreign forces, and urged the Council to take advantage of any opportunity which would promote a peaceful solution. The resolution was nothing more than a referendum for British policy outside the League; with six abstentions, but no adverse votes, it was passed on to the Assembly where it failed to get the necessary unanimity. The dissenting votes were cast by two easily dismissable countries:

[1] *Freedom's Battle*, p. 44.
[2] *Survey*, 1937, II, p. 360.
[3] *Official Journal*, Committees, 1937, pp. 107–108.

Albania, a satellite of Mussolini, and Portugal, a supporter of Franco. There were also fourteen abstentions from countries which for the most part still "clung to the sentimental hope that Non-Intervention might yet produce the desired effects." [1] Britain had used the resolution as a means of soliciting support for her negotiations with Italy.

Nations have two ways of regarding international organizations: they either exert their own leadership or follow the lead of others. League involvement with the Spanish question was conditional only upon desire and while Britain's manipulations might have produced embarrassment and shame, they produced little opposition. It almost seems that in those days the only League champions were found in the British Labour Party, which however at the moment was distracted by more serious worries.

2. DISSENT IN THE LABOUR PARTY

"Fellow delegates, you may smoke," said Chairman Hugh Dalton, opening the 1937 Conference of the Labour Party (October 4). The seaside resort of Bournemouth had been chosen because of its location and because of the "good hall in which smoking was allowed." [2] Indeed the decided improvement in accommodations over the previous year's conference did appear to be somewhat more conducive to harmony and solution of problems; divisions and frustrations caused by the Civil War were still highly conspicuous but the vacant confusion so much in evidence before was absent. During the past year there had been significant shifts in opinion. The pacifism that had formerly gripped the Party was waning and Labour in a curious reversal of roles now attacked the Government not for their militarism but for their appeasement. While Labour still opposed Non-Intervention, they were by no means willing to go to war to defend the rights of the Spanish Republic. Labour's opposition was summarized in their call "arms for Spain," but after a year of war it was becoming increasingly obvious that such a slogan was quite incompatible with a parliamentary position which in effect meant "no arms for Britain." A change was overdue, but nevertheless it did come. The last time the Labour Party voted against the Service Estimates was in 1936. During July 1937 in a

---

[1] This observation in the October 4 issue of the *Times* carried with it the implication that the others, including Britain, felt differently.
[2] Dalton, p. 141.

series of Party Meetings – "forceful but never acrimonious" – Dalton
was able to persuade the Party by a vote of 45 to 39 to reverse the
recommendation of the Executive and to abstain from voting on the
Defense Estimates. If the Party continued as before, he said, what
possible answer would there be to the "accusation that we wanted
arms for Spain, but no arms for our own country?" How would one
explain Labour's position to the man who asked "Did you vote against
all means of defending us from bombers next time? Did you vote
against our having even a single anti-aircraft gun?" Thus when the
Appropriation Bill came before Commons on July 26 and 27 only eleven
opposing votes were registered (six from the Labour Party itself).
"This, in view of the strong feelings of many of our colleagues,"
proudly concluded Dalton, "was a most remarkable display of loyalty
and discipline." [1]

Inside the Labour Party however, the same frustration which produced attacks against the Government also caused a challenge to the
Labour leadership itself. Embittered by inactivity and hesitation,
Labour's militant Left launched a concerted drive to create a United
Front. "A piece of clothed nonsense" said Dalton. "A most exasperating diversion of the Party's mind and energies." [2] The campaign was
announced a couple of months after the Conference at Edinburgh.
Spearheaded by Sir Stafford Cripps and his Socialist League, including
the Communists and the Independent Labour Party, this activity
ultimately provoked a Labour Executive reminder (on January 12,
1937) that united action with the Communists and their associates was
contrary to the interests of the Labour Party and any cases which
arose would be disciplined accordingly. On January 27 the National
Executive blacklisted the Socialist League. The campaign however
continued. Publicized by a weekly *Tribune*, the movement held public
meetings, ignoring the views of the Party. Finally the Labour Executive was forced to take strong action and by June 1, 1937 membership
in the Socialist League was made incompatible with membership in the
Labour Party. It would be unfair to say that support for a United
Front extended beyond a handful of members, although this extremism,
riding the crest of Civil War sympathies, tended to open old wounds at
a time when the Labour Party vitally needed consolidation. The Trade
Union leader, Bevin, had no use for Cripps and company; a strong
advocate of Party discipline and with more than a tinge of scorn for

[1] *Ibid.*, pp. 135–137.
[2] *Ibid.*, p. 129.

Party intellectuals, he wrote (to G. D. H. Cole) "However, we shall have the storm, the large meetings, the enthusiasm and the cheering, and then just as in the case of Abyssinia, Germany, Spain and all the other big problems, it will be the trade unions who will have to do the practical work." [1] The United Front question reached its climax at Bournemouth.

In spite of rather eloquent speeches by Cripps, Laski and George R. Strauss favouring the United Front, the decision was a foregone conclusion. When Herbert Morrison spoke for the National Executive he made little attempt to veil his threats. He first appealed to reason, meeting argument with argument, proving his case historically; tolerance toward the advocates of a United Front though was at an end. "We cannot have disunity spread in the Party in the name of unity." Morrison concluded with a fatherly appeal,

I beg of them in the name of this great Party... I beg of them in the name of the future of our country and the well being of the world, to drop it, and to come into the Party as comrades helping us in the job and thereby assisting us to stop the processes of discipline that we do not want to carry further, but which they will force us to carry further if this goes on. [2]

The Party reaffirmed their rejection of the United Front by the overwhelming vote of 2,116,000 to 331,000. Most former supporters took Morrison's hint, but Cripps persisted, and a year and a half later he was finally expelled.

The 1937 Conference discussed Spain but slightly. The resolutions calling for a nation wide campaign to compel the Government to abandon Non-Intervention and restore the Spanish Republic its rights to purchase arms was passed unanimously after little debate. Most conference business dealt with internal problems: public order, distressed areas, pension plans, and agriculture. The two main problems aroused by the Civil War, rearmament and the popular front, had been settled relatively well. But while Labour was still discussing what they would do if they had power, the Government, denied this academic luxury, was occupied with the consequences and direction of their policy that October after Nyon.

---

[1] Bullock, p. 596. It should be noted that not all members of the Labour Party became aware of the menace of Fascism by the dramatic events in Spain. Bevin and his fellow trade unionists were hostile the minute Hitler had suppressed the labour unions in Germany. They hated Communism for the same reasons.

[2] *Annual Labour Report*, 1937, p. 164.

3. COUNTER PROPOSALS AND RESERVATIONS

Mussolini's state visit to Germany the last part of September convinced him more than ever that Germany was invincible. On the same day (September 28) that 650,000 jammed the Reich Sportz Platz to hear speeches of Italo-German solidarity, there was published in Rome a warning against "new diplomatic combinations which, in the guise of conversations or conference, clothe an apparent attempt to associate Italy with England and France at the eleventh hour, thus separating her from Germany on the problems of Spain and the Mediterranean." [1] Many in Britain failed to take the hint; several days later the *Times* editorialized: "there is little reason to look for destructive explanations of the event which has just been accomplished in Germany, when in the main it offered so little that a reasonable observer could reckon disturbing, and so little that he is entitled to welcome." [2]

Mussolini returned, his path strewn with laurel leaves; the goose step, dubbed *passo romano*, became compulsory in the army.

Despite their outward solidarity Chamberlain still hoped to split Italy from Germany. Finalizing plans for a three power conference on October 2, the British Ambassador, with the French *Chargé d'Affaires*, handed Italy a joint dispatch. Friendly and conciliatory, taking the Nyon Agreement as point of departure, the note stressed the need for improving the international situation through an agreement over Spain, reminding Mussolini of British and French interest in the continuance of Non-Intervention, and saying that it was impossible to expect any progress unless the problem of volunteers were solved. Remaining alone with Ciano after the departure of the French *Chargé d'Affaires*, Drummond expressed his deep regret at the progressive deterioration of relations between their two countries, mentioning specifically Mussolini's congratulatory telegram to Franco and Italy's refusal to participate in the Nyon Conference as two of the main reasons for the present crisis; personally he reaffirmed his Government's desire to re-establish mutual friendship.[3]

Mussolini on vacation at Rocca delle Caminate was in no hurry to reply. Keeping the Germans informed, the Italians leisurely drafted an answer. On October 6th the postponement of the meeting of the

---

[1] *Times*, September 29, 1937.
[2] *Ibid.*, September 30, 1937.
[3] *Ciano's Diplomatic Papers*, p. 137.

Fascist Grand Council created speculation that Mussolini might possibly be re-examining his whole Spanish policy. The next day when Drummond and Jules Blondel, French *Chargé d'Affaires*, asked Ciano for an answer to their note, they were told that as soon as Berlin agreed on a reply Britain and France would be informed; thus did Ciano deliberately try to give an impression of Axis solidarity.[1]

Meanwhile the Conservatives were holding their annual conference at Scarborough. Lord Plymouth, explaining measures now being taken with Italy, expressed his country's desire to return to the good relations which existed between Italy and Britain before the Ethiopian war. Chamberlain voiced the Government's impatience with the Italian delay in answering the note of the 2nd, and added, "if we could once make real progress in the settlement of the Spanish problem the way would be opened to those conversations which formed the subject of the recent correspondence between Signor Mussolini and myself." [2]

Chamberlain's hopes were soon shattered; on October 9 Ciano gave Drummond and Blondel Italy's rejection. Blondel was rather upset but Drummond, showing no emotion, even asked for the name of a medicine against rheumatism, recommended earlier by Ciano, which seemed to have helped him. "He is very English," wrote the Count. Italy's response stated that tri-partite consideration of Spain, under the present circumstances, would only result in increasing misunderstandings and complications; a general agreement could be achieved more successfully through the Non-Intervention Committee, and that Italy was not disposed to take part in any discussions in which Germany did not participate. The French had expected a reply to be *evasive*, but were extremely disappointed when it turned out to be so negative. They considered the possibility of suspending Non-Intervention pending adoption of effective enforcement measures, but refused to take action without consulting Whitehall. The resultant discussions found the British far more conciliatory than the French. Chamberlain, consciously wanting to save the situation, agreed that a return to the Non-Intervention Committee might produce results. France reluctantly acquiesced. The question of opening the Franco-Spanish frontier was delayed again as the two countries emphasized that they would not tolerate any further prolonged discussions on the question of volunteers. In a speech at Llandudno on October 15th, Eden explained that France and Britain consented to have this matter again referred to the Non-

[1] Ciano, *Journal Politique*, p. 43.
[2] *Times*, October 9, 1937.

Intervention Committee because they did not want a breakdown on a possible procedural issue. He said though that this did not mean "that we are prepared to acquiescence in dilatory tactics." Distinguishing between Non-Intervention and indifference, Eden remarked,

We are not indifferent to the maintenance of the territorial integrity of Spain. We are not indifferent to the foreign policy of any future Spanish Government. We are not indifferent to the complications which may arise in the Mediterranean as the result of the intervention of others in Spain. We are not indifferent to vital British interests in the Mediterranean, a clear distinction must be made between Non-Intervention in what is purely a Spanish affair and Non-Intervention where British interests are at stake.[1]

Lloyd George felt that Eden did not go far enough. In a speech the next day at Caernarvon he censured the Government's incessant willingness to bow to the demands of Mussolini, to take a position only to abandon it later. He advised Eden to "take the course which his conscience dictates, boldly, fearlessly, dauntlessly, whatever his colleagues may say"; if he would stop being bullied by the men around him stood up for what he really believed, he would find himself the biggest man in Great Britain.[2]

Unconvinced at British determination, Ciano was surprised that the British Cabinet should have accepted the Italian rejection so mildly. "After the threats of the last few days," he wrote on the 14th, "this Anglo-French retreat leads one to reflect on the decline of the two nations." [3]

At the Non-Intervention Sub-Committee meeting on October 16 France introduced a five point plan, resembling Britain's July proposal, which called for the immediate withdrawal of volunteers, followed by the granting of belligerent rights, adding that:

the Governments represented on the Committee should exercise all their influence in Valencia and Salamanca to insure that in a very short time a definite number of volunteers should be withdrawn from each side.

and that:

arrangements should be made to insure that there should be no new departure of volunteers from any country to Spain.[4]

Count Grandi, Italy's representative, in a long speech said that the beginning of an agreement should be made by the "partial withdrawal

1 Eden, pp. 220–221.
2 *Guardian*, October 22, 1937.
3 Ciano, *Journal Politique*, p. 46.
4 *Times*, October 18, 1937.

of a certain number of volunteers in equal quantity," also stating that since Non-Intervention affairs must necessarily involve negotiations with the two Spanish parties, the recognition of them as belligerent was implicit, and "those who declare themselves in favour of Non-Intervention, but against recognition of belligerent rights cannot be considered as neutrals in respect of the Spanish conflict." [1] Grandi deliberately sought to deadlock the proceedings. Three days later he further complicated matters by suggesting the French proposals be abandoned, substituting the British plan of July 14th instead as a basis of discussion. The German delegate supported Grandi, but was clearly displeased and suggested that German influence be exerted in Rome to change Grandi's instructions.[2] There was no sense in becoming involved in petty matters of procedure; appearing conciliatory in the beginning would make it easier to remain uncompromising later on more important issues. On the 20th, Grandi, under new instructions, announced that his Government was now ready to consider taking positive steps toward the withdrawal of all volunteers. In a calculated departure from the original British plan, Grandi, changing tactics, now insisted a commission establish the exact number of volunteers on each side. This was still another screen behind which Italy could continue her dilatory tactics, but Eden remarked that if the next meeting of the Non-Intervention Committee made as much progress as the one just held the problem would very be largely solved.

Meanwhile, Opposition attacks on the Government for tolerating Italian delay increased: Non-Intervention was one-sided, and the Government failed to stand up to international Fascism. Moreover, Mussolini's blunt admission of having 40,000 of his nationals in Spain provoked demands that the Government give Italy a two week deadline to withdraw. In Commons October 21, Chamberlain dismissed such bellicosity as completely divorced from reality and expressed his faith in the Non-Intervention Committee to produce a favourable solution. Answering a political opponent, he replied,

So, instead of taunting us with truckling to dictators and with weakness in not breaking off negotiations if the Italian Government could not see their way to accept the invitation to the Three-Power Conversations, instead of denouncing us for consenting to discuss this matter once again in the Non-Intervention Committee, he has had to take up different ground altogether and to throw doubts upon the good faith of the Italian Government. The right honourable Gentleman is quite entitled to have his suspicions. All I would say is that if in

[1] *Ibid.*
[2] *GD.,* p. 470.

foreign affairs you are always going to begin with the assumption that the other party is not going to hold to anything that he promises, you will not make much progress.

The next day Grandi modified his position again, claiming that Italy was willing to reach an agreement only if the British plan were unanimously accepted by the other members of the Non-Intervention Committee. As had been expected, the Russians refused to accept a plan putting recognition of belligerency before the withdrawal of *all* volunteers. Rather than letting the Russians hold up progress on the issue of belligerency, Britain left the impression she would proceed without them. Grandi said that although his Government would agree to sending a commission to Spain, it did not mean that their findings would be necessarily binding. It was of course useless to send a commission under these conditions. Grandi finally conceded but it meant nothing. Though the Russians later accepted Britain's proviso on belligerent rights, the Italians and Germans found new provisions to be qualified, phrases to be redefined and propositions to be studied. Italy would not withdraw her troops until the end of the war and Britain did not see it to her interest to insist.

4. INDIGNANT RESIGNATION

The negotiations which continued in the Non-Intervention Committee until its end are long and drawn out, impossibly boring, and add nothing to what has already been said; their inclusion can best be handled summarily. On November 4th enough objections were removed to secure adherence, at least on the surface, to the British plan of withdrawal. When the two powers in Spain were asked their cooperation, neither was willing to give unqualified acceptance, although both agreed enough to give the Non-Intervention Committee a basis for further plans and proposals. During December the Non-Intervention Committee discussed various schemes on sending commissions to Spain. The Committee always had the most success with technicalities, because it was never taken seriously that they would go into effect, but a vital question, such as the meaning of "substantial withdrawal" or the stage at which belligerent rights would be granted, proved impossible to resolve. Italy insisted that she would only consent to a withdrawal, man for man. To end this obstacle, private talks were carried out by Lord Plymouth directly with Italy at the end of January

1938, but they produced no results. It was these talks which prompted Italy to make the suggestion that Britain and herself should enter directly into negotiation to resolve their differences.[1]

During the next two months the Non-Intervention Committee took on the aspect of an arithmatic class. Would the minimum number of initial withdrawals be 10,000 or 20,000? How many volunteers were on each side in Spain? Further difficulties. The French insisted that restoring control over their Spanish border should coincide only with the beginning of actual withdrawal; the Italians wanted it restored simultaneously with the arrival of the counting commissions. (It was no secret that the removal of the International supervision of the Franco Spanish border had been followed by French violation of Non-Intervention.) The mathematics began again. The Italians accused the French of delivering 8,096 tons of war material plus 330 aeroplanes to the Republic. On May 4th the British persuaded France to consent to a restoration of control on her Southern border, but agreement on volunteers was as far away as ever, and Italian-French relations, an important element in the British appeasement policy, were poisoned hopelessly. So much failure made the littlest concessions appear as triumphs. That the British, French, German and Italian Governments paid their fiscal obligations was interpreted as meaning they "were all in earnest in their intention to make the arrangements work so far as that lay in their power." [2]

At the meeting of July 5, 1938, a new British plan for the withdrawal of volunteers was unanimously accepted. But its final implementation depended upon its acceptance by both Spanish Governments. With no cause for worry, the Germans had made the gesture of acceptance in order to keep Chamberlain's position in his own government secure. Said a wire from Spain to the Wilhelmstrasse:

> A way must be sought, on the one hand, to strengthen Chamberlain's position by accepting the plan in principle but, on the other hand by means of skillful questions and counter proposals to win as much time as possible in order to prosecute the war in the meantime.[3]

The Italians advised Franco delay his answer to the latest volunteer plan, and over a month later Britain received a reply. As usual the scheme was accepted only "in principle," containing obviously unacceptable demands. (i.e. that belligerent rights should be uncon-

---

[1] See Chapter VII.
[2] *Survey*, 1938, I, p. 324.
[3] *GD.*, p. 725.

ditionally granted in advance of withdrawal and that equal numbers should be drawn from both sides). There was no action until the end of September when unexpectedly the impasse was seemingly broken by Juan Negrin's unilateral announcement at Geneva to withdraw all foreign combatants from the Republican army.[1] The *Times* said that the move was unquestionably politic:

> The depleted International Brigades which have fought with great courage and have sustained very heavy losses throughout the long campaign, have lately been little engaged, and their withdrawal is now unlikely to have much military importance.[2]

Shortly afterwards Franco informed Britain of his decision to evacuate a group of 10,000 Italians. Mussolini took all the credit, but was very angry when the press represented it as a concession. Franco desired to avoid future complications by getting rid of foreign troops for which he had no more use. His decision, taken before the Loyalist announcement, was in no way influenced by it or by action in the Non-Intervention Committee. Actually, Hitler had wanted to increase his military and diplomatic support in order to improve his position after victory, and Mussolini on August 20, proudly proclaiming that it was his custom to stand by his comrade to the end, proposed

1. The dispatch of two or three more divisions.
2. The dispatch of 10,000 more men to compensate for the losses in the two divisions that were already in Spain.
3. Partial or complete withdrawal of the Italians.[3]

Franco preferred partial withdrawal which still left four equipped Italian divisions. Mussolini also profited from this withdrawal which brought the Anglo-Italian pact into force.[4] Nobody mentioned the London Committee.

The Non-Intervention Committee, rightly termed a farce, was molded by the interest of the powers. Germany and Italy used the Committee to stalemate Britain who was concerned with intervention only in so far as it reflected on the containment of the war. Not expecting the Committee to prevent the transportation of arms, Britain hoped that results in the Committee would follow from outside negotiations; as she was undeceived by the intervention of Hitler and Mussolini, her reasons for continuous toleration cannot alone be found in studying Non-Intervention. This leads us first to a consideration of her business interests, and later to a study of her negotiations with Italy.

[1] See Chapter VIII, part 2.
[2] *Times*, September 29, 1938.
[3] *GD.*, pp. 765–766.
[4] See Chapter VIII, part 2.

CHAPTER VI

STRUGGLE FOR SPANISH RECOURCES

I. BRITISH BUSINESS INTERESTS

Conditioned by their Victorian antecedents, the British business class had no attachment to either war or idealism. Both were bad for trade. Accustomed to social continuity at home, they were repelled by disintegration abroad. From their experiences, acquired to some degree through their own imposition of order on foreigners, they recognized the existence of stability to be a prerequisite for all profitable activity and progress. Therefore, their tendency to favour authoritarianism was strong and led them to favour Franco.

The natural resources of Spain had attracted British interests long before July 1936. As one of Spain's best customers, she consistently took about half of her total exports and supplied her in turn with almost one fifth of her imports; her direct investment in the Spanish economy, chiefly concentrated in mining public utilities and public works, was extensive. The iron ore deposits in the Cantabrian Mountains were originally owned and developed by British finance; the development of copper mining at Rio Tinto and Tharsis was also due to her capital; the Barcelona Traction, Light and Power Company, the Seville Waterworks, and the Anglo-Spanish Rail Road Construction Company, largely in British hands, testify to her financial diversity. Although direct purchases were mostly confined to strategic metals, Britain still was a heavy buyer of Spanish wheat as well as bitter oranges, almonds, potatoes, tobacco and wine.[1] Although small in terms of total trade, the Spanish market was not insignificant and the losses due to the war not inconsiderable.

[1] *Statesman's Year Book*, 1938, p. 1325; *Survey*, 1937, II, pp. 170–171.

Table 1: Total Trade of Britain with Spain.[1]

	1934	1935	1936	1937	1938
Imports into Britain . . .	11,263	11,119	10,515	8,510	5,733
Exports to Spain	4,794	5,344	2,975	2,444	3,455

(In thousands of £s)

Table 2: Percentage of Spanish Trade with Total Trade.[2]

	1934	1935	1936	1937	1938
Imports	1.54	1.47	1.24	0.83	0.62
Exports	1.07	1.11	0.59	0.41	0.65

Thus as compared with two pre-war years, exports show a drop of about 50% as contrasted with 41% for imports.

The outbreak of the war immediately affected British exports. Both Spanish Governments were interested primarily in importing materials of war, which, not supplied by Britain, were bought in Russia by the Loyalists and in Germany by the Nationalists. From the point of view of both imports and exports, 1937 was the year of heaviest loss. The following year the tide somewhat turned, showing either less comparative loss or an advance. British exports by their very nature were more conductive to long run trade than were those of Germany. In 1937 her chief exports, in order of importance, were: coal, cotton yarns, chemical products, iron and steel manufacturers, machinery, and coke, while Germany concentrated mostly on ammunition and weapons of destruction.

In terms of her Spanish imports, Britain generally suffered more in the field of agriculture than raw materials.

Table 3: Leading Imports from Spain during the War.[3]

A. Raw Materials . .	1936	1937	1938
Iron Ore	971,913	1,118,746	702,970
Mercury	222,009	418,658	437,586
Pyrites	224,101	380,967	382,669
B. Agriculture . . .	1936	1937	1938
Oranges	2,117,907	1,709,561	975,082
Potatoes	1,075,752	460,394	220,905
Almonds	728,757	678,345	589,715

(In thousands of gold pesetas)

[1] *Statesman's Year Book*, 1938, p. 1334.
[2] Calculated from figures in Table 1 and total trade figures in the *Statistical Summary of the Bank of England*, February 1939.
[3] *Statesman's Year Book*, 1938, p. 1325; 1940, p. 1302.

When one examines the statistics of this period it should be remembered that they are constitued for Spain as a whole. British business tried to remain apolitical, working with the changing territorial situation as best as it could, in terms of past economic interests. At first the existence of an Anglo-Spanish Payments Agreement while making trade with the Loyalists more difficult, paralyzed it with the Nationalists. Therefore, until this matter was resolved, the loss of trade, shown in collective figures, has to be assumed as coming more from the Nationalist side than the Loyalist. On the Republican side the absence of dangerous competition enabled Britain to maintain a leading position. In the first quarter of 1937 exports fell very little when one considers that before the war there were 33,510,000 gold pesetas of export to all of Spain and in early 1937 20,454,000 to Loyalist Spain alone,[1] Later, as machinery, electrical appliances, motor cars and chemicals were prohibited for export and as more territory fell to Franco, the picture changed.

The statistics have shown that British imports fell less than her exports, and that the heaviest loss in imports was in agriculture. Certainly much of this loss was due to diversion and neglect, but that is not the whole story. Early in the war the Germans tried to capitalize on the trade vacuum between Britain and the Insurgents in order to divert the entire orange crop in Andalusia to Germany. By reason of this example and the fact that conditions in Nationalist Spain were relatively orderly, it would be safe to infer that losses to Britain in export of oranges were strongly influenced by German pressure. Furthermore, Franco's strategy of war mirrored German and Italian desires, which usually considered the economic significance of the area to be attacked. This motivation was behind the thrust towards Cordoba, the richest mineral area in Spain with the world's most abundant deposits of mercury, and was also the case in the moves on Bilbao, one of the largest and most accessible iron ore areas in Europe.

At the beginning of the war it was thought the Italians were interested largely in mercury. Their capture of Malaga early in 1937 opened the approach to Cordoba, where lay the largest deposits of this mineral. Italy, being with Spain the largest producer of mercury in the world, naturally made people assume that by her seizure of the Spanish mines she was making an attempt to corner the world's supply. But in view of the fact that British imports of Spanish mercury actually increased during the war, her attempt does not appear to have been too successful

[1] *The Economist*, February 12, 1938.

and indicates that Italy, unlike the Germans, possessed neither the skill nor the organization from which to force concessions. Although their imports from Spain were insignificant when compared to the large quantities of wheat, wool, hides, skins, olive oil, sugar, ores and pyrites which had reached Germany, the war did occasion a sharp increase in certain commodities. During the first six months of 1937, before the capture of Bilbao, the movement of raw materials to Italy amounted to only 5,116 tons, whereas in the following two months it jumped to 23,192. However, Italy's principal item of import was not strategic metals, but rather olive oil, which during the first eight months of 1937 reached 5,624 metric tons.[1]

Moreover, there not only was anticipated interruption and destruction due to actual fighting, but there existed, more dangerous in the long run, an indirect struggle for control. Influenced by certain assumptions (that the Spanish character would not tolerate foreign interference after the war and that Britain was the only country capable of providing necessary capital for inevitable reconstruction), the British Government was slow to examine the consequences of a Republican defeat. Nevertheless such an appraisal was mandatory.

2. THE INDIRECT WAR

During the summer of 1937 victories in the Basque country left the Insurgents controlling a majority of Spanish provinces, which, from the British point of view, were geographically the most important. In private, Eden had told Delbos that he frankly preferred a Rebel victory because he believed "Great Britain could make an agreement with Franco which would ensure the departure of Germans and Italians from Spain." [2] The necessity to come to terms with Franco, thus stated by such a high Government official was a step toward recognition, and, with the gradual extension of Nationalist territory, the British Government began "exerting its subtle powers of propaganda towards gently preparing public opinion" for this eventuality.[3] (Labour feared that the Government, taking advantage of the summer recess of Parliament in 1937, would extend recognition behind their back.) A further factor compelling this readjustment was the preferential treatment given the

[1] *USD.*, 1937, I, pp. 443–444.
[2] *Ibid.*, p. 369.
[3] *Ibid.*, p. 375.

Germans on mineral concessions, largely as a direct result of military pressure. The capitulation of Bilbao showed German intentions to be little different from practices elsewhere (i.e. the desire to involve Spain in large raw material commitments, extremely difficult to break, promoting dependence on the German economy.) Previously, Germany had confined her activity to Central and South Eastern Europe; she had undercut markets and disrupted them, causing damage to the foreign trade of others. In Danube countries, where her interests were minimal, overall loss to Britain was slight, but Spain was a different story.

Early in the war Franco had confiscated the Rio Tinto mines in Andalusia, supposedly redirecting their deposits of copper, pyrites and sulphur to other points in Spain. In practice however, this meant that what had formerly gone to Britain was now being transferred to Germany and Italy. To prevent the complete loss of so strategic an area, British private interests on January 15, 1937 proposed an agreement whereby the output of the mines would be divided, 40% to Britain, the rest to Germany and Spain. In rejecting this plan, the Nationalist Government, claiming the company was under Spanish law, said that "the Spanish Government explicitly reserved for itself full freedom of action distributing ... production." [1] (Germany subsequently received a promise for 60% of the total production.) Having received no satisfaction at an unofficial level, the British on February 4, 1937, through their Berlin Embassy, directly approached the Germans, informing them that the British Government was supporting the claim of the Rio Tinto Company for compensation, because they considered the seizure an illegal act in which Germany was involved through their acceptance of the confiscated copper.[2] Four days later, the British Embassy was told that the matter concerned private transaction and as such did not concern the German Government. (An obvious lie on two counts: first, because of the very nature of Germany's totalitarian society and second, because of the control exercised in Spain by the monopolistic company Hisma-Rowak. This latter organization, being the means through which German penetration of Spain was effected, enjoyed a semi-diplomatic status. It had its birth on August 27, 1937, when Franco established a company, called "Hisma Limitado, Carranza y Bernhardt," to control all raw material output from mines in Morocco. However, the real powers lay in the German branch called

[1] GD., p. 230.
[2] Ibid., p. 240.

"Rowak" in Berlin and the scope of its operations spread to all mineral resource under Insurgent control.) Ensuing negotiations between British and Germans firms were inconclusive, and in July the claim was definitely rejected.

German intervention was related directly to Franco's cooperation in fulfilling raw material demands. "Although we did not wish to make our procurement of raw materials strictly a condition for our services to General Franco," said the German Economic Policy Director, "the latter would nevertheless admit that in view of our own limited potentialities our services to him were to a certain extent dependent on our essential imports from Spain." [1] This policy cut two ways; while increasing Spanish dependence on Germany, it made Franco uneasy about German ambitions.

Most British capital investment was concentrated in areas held by the Loyalist Government, and remained so until late in the war; but British security depended more on raw materials than on investments. While businessmen feared losing income from investment as much as losing markets, the Government was chiefly concerned with losing primary products. Britain, it should be remembered, was undergoing rearmament, which intensified competition for all strategic materials. This struggle was dramatically reflected in the price levels of the London commodity market. Speculation was rampant, in a year nonferrous metals almost doubled their 1936 quotations; copper, its output severely curtailed by the Civil War, climbed to its highest level since 1929. The refineries in South Wales, already an area of unemployment, had to close for lack of ore, and, in the summer of 1937, with Franco in control of the iron ore deposits of Northern Spain, the situation promised to be more serious than ever. Germany's concern over British competition in the Swedish ore fields and a contemplated French embargo of reserves in Lorraine made her lose little time in obtaining as much Spanish ore as possible; by the end of 1936 she had a large shipping fleet under the protection of her navy employed in transporting ore to her smelters. Spanish iron exports to Germany rose from a December 1936 level of 37,210 tons to 206,707 tons the following January.[2] "It is not too much to say," said one observer, "that the German adventure in Spain saved the German rearmament programme". [3] As soon as the control of the Basque iron deposits passed into the

[1] Ibid., p. 288.
[2] The Economist, May 15, 1937.
[3] New Statesman, April 24, 1937.

hands of Franco, German ships arrived, their holds eager for further consignments.

Britain was accustomed to import on the average about a million tons of Spanish ore a year. The quality of the Basque ore was liked because of its high iron content, which considerably increased the efficiency of their blast furnaces. At first the war worked in Britain's favour. The Basques, isolated from the rest of the Republic, sent virtually their entire output to Britain. This situation immediately changed after their surrender, and what used to come in quantity became a trickle. On July 11, 1937, a broadcast from Seville gave a clear warning that "the Nationalists could not guarantee the mining property of nationals of states that were unwilling to give General Franco's Government diplomatic recognition." [1] Deliveries were provisionally stopped and not until the end of August were they resumed with an ore delivery to Cardiff. Early in September 1937, Franco sounded out the British on an exchange of agents. In a dispatch transmitted through their Hendaye [2] diplomatic post Britain said she regarded this proposal favourably providing the agents dispatched were of semi-official character, enjoying the rights and duties of a consul, but not possessing his diplomatic privileges; final consent was made contingent upon the solution of certain problems: "release of certain British ships, unhampered activity of British consuls in Nationalist Spain, and solution of some economic questions." [3]

The Germans knew it was impossible to keep England from the Spanish market; a foreign ministry report said:

Even if we may assume that General Franco does not intend to satisfy England's wishes to the detriment of German's interests, nevertheless any negotiations by Spain with a third country are potentially dangerous to the position of preeminence which we have won in Spain in the economic field. This is especially true with relation to England; for German and British interests, as is well known, confront one another on Spanish soil, particularly in the case of iron ores, which are especially important for Germany, and also in the case of copper and pyrites, so that it requires a special effort to maintain as long and as fully as possible the pre-eminence we have won with regard to these raw materials.[4]

[1] Survey, 1937, II, p. 175.
[2] Early in the war Britain had moved their Embassy to St. Jean de Luz (shortly afterwards to Hendaye where it stayed until the Republican defeat) in France, leaving a Chargé d' Affaires in Madrid. When the Republic moved their capital to Valencia, Britain considered withdrawing all diplomatic representation from Madrid, but following a protest from the British colony who chose to stay in the besieged city, this plan was abandoned. During the course of the war the Embassy buildings became barracks for political refugees. The British absence of an Ambassador in Madrid was explained in the Commons by Baldwin on 29 October 1936.
[3] GD., p. 455.
[4] Ibid., p. 461.

Germany was determined to safeguard supplies of raw materials; a secret protocol had been already negotiated with Franco on July 12, 1937, guaranteeing that any comprehensive economic negotiations would be held first with Germany. But Germany did not trust the word of Franco and lived in constant fear that she would be gradually forced out of the Spanish market.

The talks at Hendaye between the British Embassy and Franco's representatives had meanwhile come to the attention of the Opposition and on November 4, in the Commons, Attlee asked whether the Government had decided to accord *de facto* recognition to the Spanish Insurgents, and if so, what were its circumstances and implications. Chamberlain, stating that there would be no change in the attitude or policy of Non-Intervention, replied that the Government had nevertheless to consider its responsibilities for protecting British nationals and commercial interests.[1] "It has become increasingly evident," he continued,

that the numerous questions affecting British interests in these areas cannot be satisfactorily delt with by means of the occasional contacts which have hitherto existed. Accordingly, His Majesty's Government have entered upon negotiations for the appointment of agents by them and by General Franco respectively for the discussion of questions affecting British nationals and commercial interests, but these agents will not be given any diplomatic status.

The debates which followed four days later revealed the whole gamut of class hostility, from the Communist Billy Gallacher:

The interests of the people of this country are more important than any commercial and financial interests. I again assert that these financial and commercial interests are the interests of members of the Cabinet. Let them have the courage to stand up and admit it.

to the head of the Independent Labour Party Jimmie Maxton:

British national prestige and British public money and British public servants should not be used for petty little jobs for commercialists in Spain, either in the Franco territory or the Government territory.

Eden denied the Government's action contained any ulterior motive. In view of the losses to commerce as a result of the war the arrangement

---

[1] In Rome two days later in conversation with Ribbentrop Mussolini said: "There is no doubt that London realizes it has backed the losing horse, and is now trying out a rapid change of attitude towards Nationalist Spain. Italy and Germany must be very much on their guard, because the problem is of particular interest to us from two points of view: financial and political ... the financial aspect of the problem is linked with the political one – only if Spain remains within our system will we be able to count on complete idemnification." *Ciano's Diplomatic Papers*, p. 144. Mussolini claimed that by the above date Italy had spent in Spain some four and a half lira to three and a half for Germany. (94.90 lire = 1 pound).

was concluded practically and reasonably in the interests of British trade. Attlee was not entirely convinced; he said:

The whole of this business causes in our minds the greatest suspicion. Although it is not recognition *de facto* or *de jure* it is a kind of half way house towards it. It has given General Franco satisfaction... In view of the whole record of the past eighteen months, we cannot take the Right Honorable Gentleman's protestations at their face value. In spite of Dr. Jekyll we shall vote against Mr. Hyde.

But in spite of Mr. Attlee, the motion was passed and followed by an exchange of agents.

The Government's policy was sound. Although the general Spanish policy was little affected by commercial interests, without an agent in Nationalist Spain it was impossible to protest against the harm done to Britain's commercial interests. There obviously were political considerations; however, according to Chamberlain, the British Government by reason of the hostile criticism from the Left Wing in the country "had based their action on commercial rather than political grounds." [1] The business approach was less dramatic than diplomatic victory, but it proved to be a lasting success.

3. RECOGNITION IN FACT

Political sympathy aside, one can not read the sources of the time without feeling a certain admiration for Franco; he might have been disastrous for the solution of his own country's problems, but his success in handling foreigners can not be denied. He skilfully played on their interests and their rivalries, and even in Britain among men who were revolted by everything for which Franco stood, there was a certain amount of deference. With no matter whom he dealt, Franco was desirous of retaining freedom of action. In early 1937 he had forced the non-confiscated British companies to either surrender all their output or deposit its full value in pounds sterling prior to export. (From the standpoint of foreign exchange it was much wiser for him to control the output this way than it was to expropriate the company). The companies were naturally displeased, but preferring half a pie to none at all, were willing to cooperate rather than risk seizure. Payments were made in Nationalist pesetas (only to 80% of value, the remaining percentage being supplied by forced credit) at a rate of exchange almost

[1] *Documents on British Foreign Policy*, II, p. 298.

twice that quoted on the free market.[1] In February 1937, Franco announced that credits received from British exports should be spent on local Spanish goods, but gave no assurance that trade would be guaranteed. He tried to keep all promises unofficial, and actual guarantees to minimum. On October 9th, 1937 he issued a decree suspending "all acts disposing of mining property, or the purchase, sale, or transfer of shares in mining companies or leases" and voiding "all titles to mining property, leases, exchanges, sales or purchase of material, or of properties used in the exploitation of mines or the immediate processing of their products, obtained since July 18, 1936." [2] This obviously slapped the German face as much as the British, and it was not long before Berlin complained Spain was being uncooperative.

Insisting upon equality of rights, German representatives were evasively told by General Jordana that the treaties which had been signed between Germany and Spain were surely to be understood "as meaning the Spanish laws would always be observed." [3] Göring was infuriated; on the basis of supposedly reliable reports, he was convinced that Franco was granting major concessions to the British behind his back. Feeling that Franco was directly indebted to him for all his "unusually great personal assistance" he assumed the right to make specific demands regarding the "war booty," and he wanted Von Jagwitz, a Hisma-Rowak official, to proceed at once to Salamanca "to hold a pistol to General Franco's breast..." Von Jagwitz, however, unsure of Franco's reaction, urged circumspection. Certain things, he wrote were no doubt

under way between Franco and England which we regarded as suspicious, if only for the reason that Franco did not put his cards on the table in these matters, but it should not be overlooked that Franco quite naturally had to take British commercial interests in Spain into account.[4]

A cautious attitude was adopted; Göring though did insist, over the objections of the Embassy, in having his own personal representative in Spain to secure Germany's economic position. This was still no guarantee. On November 30th Franco's concessions to Britain appeared much larger than had been originally suspected. Instructing their Spanish Ambassador, Von Neurath said:

Naturally, we recognize the necessity, as already stated in the instruction of October 16, of letting England also have a share in the trade with Spain. But we

[1] *Survey*, 1937, II, p. 173.
[2] *GD.*, p. 457.
[3] *Ibid.*
[4] *Ibid.*, p. 509.

will by no means put up with a favouring of England which displaces us from our economic position, especially in the purchase of raw materials. If General Franco should reply evasively or indeed confirm the correctness of our information, at the same time refusing to give satisfactory explanations as to how he will give our justified interests their due, please inform him plainly that in this case we on our part shall unfortunately be forced to re-examine our attitude toward the Spanish Nationalist Government on various questions in view of this new situation.[1]

Although claiming concessions to Britain as pure fabrications, Franco made no move to satisfy German demands. When they presented him with requests for mining rights he talked ambigously about compatability with old Spanish laws; when they showed displeasure, he placidly asked for more military aid. The Germans were finally forced to conclude that no amount of pressure would succeed; they therefore emphasized the general development of common political, economic and ideological objectives.

Meanwhile, by December 1937 the commercial agents had assumed their duties. Franco's representative was the Duke of Alba, a Spanish Grandee with Scottish-English ancestry; educated at Beaumont College, Windsor and long in the habit of making annual trips to Britain, his appointment seemed entirely appropriate and at the first opportunity Alba expressed pleasure at the resumption of commercial relations between Britain and Spain. It was not long before this activity attracted the attention of Germany and Italy. The Italians, skeptically regarding the exchange, were not gratified to hear Alba praise England so extravagantly as Spain's best customer. Germany was of like mind; their Ambassador in Spain thought that Alba was trying through his connections "to work for England and to create sentiment against German and Italian influence in Spain." [2]

Britain had sent to Insurgent Spain the capable diplomat, Sir Robert Hodgson; in spite of Chamberlain's previous contradictions, Hodgson upon arrival was immediately accorded full diplomatic privileges. Before Hodgson's appointment extensive contact had already existed between the Hendaye Embassy and Franco's Government. The British Commercial Attaché, Pack, was a frequent visitor to Burgos and Salamanca, discussing economic questions. Ambassador Henry Chilton, accredited to the Republic, maintained active diplomatic intercourse with the Rebels. Every day he sent notes and telegrams. On one occasion an important speech given by Eden in the House of Commons at

[1] *Ibid.*, p. 518.
[2] *Ibid.*, p. 533.

3 o'clock in the afternoon, had been summarized by Chilton for Franco at 10 o'clock that same morning. There is no evidence to suggest that Chilton acted on the direct instructions of the British Government, but the Germans seem to have assumed he had.[1] Considerable liaison existed between the British Embassy at Hendaye and Hodgson in the performance of his duties, but, contrary to the Embassy's feeling that it was more prudent to stay as close to the frontier as possible, Hodgson proceeded directly to the Insurgent Capital. He disliked their suggestion for several reasons: it would have made contact with Nationalist officials impossible, increased the difficulty in obtaining reliable information, and have created the impression of being under the general direction of an Embassy accredited to the Republic. (This should have made little difference for, according to the American Ambassador, Claude Bowers, the British Ambassador Chilton was already violently pro-Franco. Every action he took had been "transparently intended to cripple the [Republican] Government and to serve the insurgents." In a characteristic statement Chilton said, "I hope they send in enough Germans to end the war.") [2] On December 16th, Hodgson and his small staff motored directly to Salamanca where they established themselves in the Grand Hotel. They were greeted by the chief of Franco's Diplomatic Cabinet and his secretary, both Spanish noblemen; on the night of his arrival Hodgson expressed the desire that his mission be received with the friendly disposition which would contribute to the "re-establishment of the normal relations of confidence and understanding that have existed for centuries between Spain" and Great Britain. The *Times* correspondent commented that "Sir Robert created an excellent impression... by saluting in the Nationalist manner during the playing of the Spanish National anthem." [3] (Sir Robert denied making the salute). Several days later the British delegation was taken to Burgos where they made acquaintance with several Government ministers, including General Jordana. Through subsequent contacts Hodgson was able to learn Spanish opinion about his country's policy and contrary to what had been hoped, nowhere was there gratitude for British Non-Intervention. Among Nationalists who regarded the war as a crusade, there was the definite tendency to associate Britain with all enemies who were conspiring "to subject Spain to a revolting Communist tyranny, massacring the people and repudiating her most sacred

---

[1] *Ibid.*, pp. 200–201.
[2] *USD.*, 1937, I, pp. 224–225.
[3] *Times*, December 20, 1937.

doctrines and tenents." [1] There was annoyance at the insistence with which the British considered the "Saviours of Spain" as Insurgents; and her refusal to grant belligerent rights was regarded as criminally absurd. "Britain, by refusing to honour in practice the precepts she applauded in theory, was responsible for the demolition of Spanish towns, the needless prolongation of the Civil War and the loss of many Spanish lives." [2]

There were, however, certain mitigating factors. Anglophiles, like the Duke of Alba, who had either gone to school in England or had had favourable contact with England in other ways, were by no means rare. Moreover, in some respects Hodgson came to Spain at a propitious time. The Italians had discredited themselves, both in prowess of arms and manners; and the Germans, by their continual insistence on financial and raw material compensation, their surreptitious meddling in Spanish interests, had considerably spoiled an initial popularity. Their sacrifices were judged insignificant compared to those made by the Spaniards themselves, supposedly unmotivated by selfish considerations of international politics. When the Falangist Government moved to Burgos, the smallness of the town and the absence of proper accommodations gave Franco a convenient opportunity to restrict their influence. While the British delegation obtained an office overlooking the Cathedral Square and living quarters in the town's centre, the German and Italian ambassadors were obliged to take up residence at San Sebastian, some 280 kilometres away. Hodgson however did not consider this arrangement as favoritism, explaining that the "British Government, in spite of its declared neutrality of outlook, was credited with strong hostility to the régime in power and our kindly treatment was to demonstrate that we were not to be penalized for it." [3] His first interview with Franco did not occur until February 1, 1938 in Salamanca. Hodgson tried to assure the Insurgent leader of the sincere nature of British neutrality, which was motivated by a genuine desire for world peace, saying that Britain desired Spain "to emerge from the Civil War united and prosperous, independent politically and territorially intact." Franco's reply was non-committal; expressing a friendly feeling toward Great Britain, he replied that when the war had begun he was

---

[1] Hodgson, p. 84.
[2] *Ibid.*, p. 85. Hostility was equally in evidence among the Loyalists, who regarded Non-Intervention as the key to Fascist intervention.
[3] *Ibid.*, p. 91.

busy learning English, for he was hoping to start very shortly for Scotland, where he intended to learn to play golf. He went on to talk of the days of Wellington, to stress the cultural bonds that united Spanish and English families and to assure me that the simple folk in Spain entertained towards Britain the kindest sentiments.[1]

Hodgson found Franco a "very attractive personality." Franco it seems had a certain dexterity in impressing the British with his sincerity and friendship while having no understanding whatsoever of their democracy. On one occasion he told Arthur Loveday, former head of the British Chamber of Commerce in Spain, that Britain's difficulties were due to her system of "Government and Press, which result in Parliament being guided by public opinion and public opinion being guided and controlled by a press which is in the hands of individual industrialists, Jews and people with definite political tendencies, who are not necessarily patriotic or primarily interested in the welfare of [the] country." Loveday called Franco "well informed as regards the political situation" in England.[2]

Britain was resigned by this time to an Insurgent victory and the duties of Hodgson increasingly assumed a political direction. He handled protests of air attacks on civilians, aided discussions on exchange of prisoners and attempted truce negotiations between Loyalist and Nationalist sympathizers. In his "unofficial" capacity he freely mixed with the diplomats of countries which had already recognized Franco; his presence in Falangist Spain demonstrated a tacit British assurance to support Franco against German encroachment. When the Czech crisis occurred in the fall of 1938, Britain and France were not disappointed to learn,

The Government of Spain intends to maintain complete neutrality in the event of the outbreak of war in Central Europe on condition that no power provokes war in Nationalist territory. Their air and armed forces will in no circumstances cross the Spanish frontier as long as Spain is not attacked.[3]

Franco's failure to inform Germany at once about this neutrality declaration was the source of much dissatisfaction in Berlin.

Franco was seldom sincere; he tricked the Germans and the Italians and, depending on his interest at the moment, he also tricked the British. Bending with the political climate, supremely xenophobic, he found German and Italian commitments uncomfortable, but he was

[1] *Ibid.*, p. 103.
[2] Loveday, pp. 112–113.
[3] Hodgson, p. 131.

not prepared to accept British friendship blindly. The presence of their Chancellery in Burgos, with the rest of the Diplomatic Corps at San Sebastian, eventually became embarrassing; and when Britain's Ambassador Sir Maurice Peterson arrived in March 1939, he was courteously but unmistakably informed "that this anomaly has to be terminated." [1] Peterson had less illusions about Franco than Hodgson and the announcement of Spain's adherence to the Anti-Comintern Pact, soon after the fall of Madrid, occasioned a clash with Jordana. When the subject was broached, Jordana stiffened and, as if reciting a lesson, said Spain "had no object in adhering other than that which the name of the instrument implied." Peterson conceded this was very reassuring but added "the motives of some at least of the other partners would not perhaps stand up equally well to examination." [2]

As soon as the war was won, Franco's dislike of foreigners became more apparent. At the slightest provocation he enjoyed summoning the Diplomatic Corps not for reasons of courtesy but because he enjoyed their presence as window dressing. After the withdrawal of their troops, Franco still was more diplomatic with the Germans than with others. By contrast Peterson found the treatment accorded British subjects highly objectionable; determined to protect British interests and subjects he admitted "on the one hand, I did not expect to find popularity ready made for Britain; on the other, I was not prepared to assume the garb of the penitent in order to obtain it." [3] This attitude contributed to his recall after the conclusion of the Anglo-Spanish Trade Agreement which following efforts made during the Civil War, was signed in March 1940. In stressing an improvement of relations through trade, this agreement marked a change from the Civil War policy of protecting British interests. Sir Samuel Hoare, Peterson's successor, claimed that it was British success in the economic field which helped keep Franco neutral, but interested in rebuilding his country, Franco had neither the desire nor the resource to fight in another war. Considering the unusual circumstances during the Civil War Britain was able to retain a surprisingly large share of the Spanish market. In dealing with Franco Britain practiced a form of appeasement, but an appeasement which was successful because it was one of mutual benefit, having its beginning in negotiation, its ultimate reinforcement in military victory.

[1] Peterson, p. 174.
[2] *Ibid.*, pp. 180–181.
[3] *Ibid.*, p. 185.

Of dictators with whom Britain had to negotiate, Franco, caring little for international glory, more Bismarckian than Napoleonic in ambition, proved comparatively reasonable. By contrast, Mussolini, a demagogue from the streets, had unlimited objectives and British statesmen found him more difficult to please and, as subsequent negotiations were to show, to understand.

CHAPTER VII

RESULTS OF VIOLATION

I. SPHERES OF SEPARATION

History convinced Mussolini that war with Britain was inevitable. Spanish intervention, although more costly than originally anticipated, did not change his opinion, nor for that matter his self confidence. Put the following epitaph on my tomb, he told Ciano: "Here lies one of the most intelligent animals to appear on the face of the earth." The belief that Britain was blocking his way to greatness made him determined to cause her humiliation. Mussolini found Eden's insistence on Non-Intervention annoying. After the failure to hold tripartite discussions, Eden suggested that Ciano meet him in Brussels. Ciano was delighted; "all the searchlights of world wide publicity," he wrote, "will concentrate on the Eden-Ciano talks." [1] But Mussolini did not consider it opportune, and the offer was coldly dismissed. Eden, tired of being continually rebuked, gave a speech in Parliament on November 1st (regarded by Ciano as very hostile) in which he said:

It is nations' foreign policies, not their internal policies, with which we are concerned. We will work wholeheartedly with other nations who are like-minded with us, and there are many such. We offer cooperation to all, but we will accept dictation from none.

Four days later Italy signed the Anti-Comintern Pact, "anti-communist in theory, but in fact unmistakably anti-British." [2] This act, a logical consequence of Italo-German co-operation in Spain, was Mussolini's way of informing Chamberlain that although he still desired negotiations with Britain, attempts to weaken the Rome-Berlin Axis would be useless. Chamberlain though continued to press for negotiations. At the London Guild Hall on November 9th he said, "We

[1] Ciano, *Journal Politique*, p. 54.
[2] *Ibid.*, p. 56.

believe that that understanding, which might well have far reaching effects in restoring confidence and security to Europe, will be more hopefully pursued by informal discussion than by public declamation." [1] Mussolini answered him the next day in an anonymous article in the *Informazione Diplomatica*, noting that "Chamberlain has ceased to believe in or hope for a weakening of the Rome-Berlin Axis." Mussolini directly referred to the Prime Ministers suggestion; "In Roman circles it is thought that one should not delay in holding conversations and reaching a conclusion through the normal diplomatic channels – a method which has always been preferred by the Fascist Government – otherwise one will be forced to believe that all this is being done to gain time, as a sort of anaesthetic. That is an error in judgment, since no one will allow himself to be chloroformed or surprised." [2] In spite of this rather theatrical bit of rhetoric it did amount to an acceptance on the part of Mussolini and consequently later that month (November 1937) and the early part of the next, conversations took place in London between Eden and Count Grandi. Concerning the Grandi-Eden talks Ciano wrote: "I have spoken with Grandi and I had to cheer him up because he was a bit worried. He does not feel an agreement with London possible. I have told him that I, to the contrary, regard it with the same optimism as before, but in any case, our situation is such that it gives us the opportunity to foresee at the same time in all calmness an eventual clash." [3] Mussolini's plans were ambitious; he wanted a complete settlement of Anglo-Italian relations with eventual recognition of his Ethiopian conquests. He most likely also envisaged a Mediterranean agreement in which he would trap the British with a limitation of armaments. But he did not feel that his desire for talks implied any diminuation of Anti-British propaganda. On December 11, occasioning Italy's withdrawal from the League of Nations, Mussolini made a bombastic speech from the Palazzo Venezia balcony. With unmistakable inference he shouted:

The good intentions of certain Governments vanish as soon as their delegates come into contact with that destructive environment represented by the Geneva Council of fools, manoevred by turbid occult forces, enemies of our Italy and of our revolution. [4]

The Italian transmitter at Bari poured out abuse, causing protests from Anthony Eden, who warned the Italian Ambassador that unless these

[1] Chamberlain, pp. 44–45.
[2] *Ciano's Diplomatic Papers*, p. 157.
[3] *Journal Politique*, p. 79.
[4] *Times*, December 13, 1937.

attacks were stopped, conversations for improving relations would be impossible. The Italian press insisted that Eden leave the Foreign Office; broadcasts mentioned that the British Empire was decadent, protected by a museum-piece fleet and that Anthony Eden was a clown in the hands of the Masons.[1]

These measures did not assure Eden that Anglo-Italian talks would accomplish anything. When (on December 23) the Italians submitted definite proposals, he delayed answering. Chamberlain, on the contrary, felt talks should begin as soon as possible. The Prime Minister fundamentally believed that no nation would deliberately design a foreign policy to lead to war. The Spanish question policy, having been reasonably handled by the Government's policy, could now be submerged in a consideration of other problems, but Eden thought Mussolini should first honour his Non-Intervention commitments before undertaking further discussion. In the Commons December 21, 1937, David Grenfell asked, "Was not the object of Non-Intervention to stop intervention?" Chamberlain corrected, "The policy was designed with the object of confining the conflict to Spain."

Meantime, during the second week of December, Clement Attlee was visiting Spain. Unofficial visits by members of Parliament to the Republican side had been rather frequent, but on no previous occasion was there to be so much controversy. As leader of the Opposition, Attlee was particularly vulnerable. He had a great admiration for the men who fought in the International Brigades, and on his trip he was persuaded to lend his name to the British contingent, henceforth named the "Major Attlee Company." He additionally expressed sympathy for the Loyalist cause to the extent of giving the clenched fist salute. As he explained later in answer to those who criticized his action, "at that time this salute was commonly used by all supporters of the Republic, whether they were Liberals, Socialists, Communists or Anarchists." [2] Of his inspection of the British Brigade, he wrote, "this was an impressive scene in a Spanish village by torchlight. The Brigade had saved the Republican cause in Spain. Serving in its ranks were men of diverse views, but animated with courage, self-sacrifice and devotion, united in the fight for freedom." [3] Attlee's supposed treason to his pledge, which all who were going to Spain had to sign in order to obtain a visa, to take no action which would compromise the British

---

[1] *Guardian*, December 31, 1937.
[2] Attlee, p. 95.
[3] *Ibid.*, p. 94.

position of Non-Intervention caused certain elements of the Conservative Party, under the prompting of Walter S. Liddall, to demand his censure. From a procedural standpoint a motion of censure on the leader of the Opposition by members of the Government is unique. Customarily this device is considered the prerogative of the Opposition to use against the Government. "I was much impressed," said Attlee, "with what I saw in Republican Spain, but not much impressed with what is being said in London." [1] In the Commons on December 13 Attlee made a personal explanation.

It cannot be too strongly emphasized that a private member of Parliament does not in his words or actions involve the British Government, but that he is a free man with the right of freely expressing his opinions ... of course, on the few occasions when I made speeches in Spain, while I abstained from criticizing the Government policy, I did state the intention of the party which I have the honour to lead, to do their utmost in every legitimate way to assist them in their struggle. I claim that, as a member of this House, I have the right to do so. I utterly repudiate the suggestion that in doing so I have broken any pledge.

Fortunately, the wiser heads among the Conservatives prevailed, and the matter was quickly dropped.

At that time the British volunteers were branded variously as fanatical and irresponsible Marxists, pathetic dupes, or heroes of the democratic faith. There was a certain amount of truth in these allegations; impelled by a desire to give their ideals reality through struggle, these men went willingly, making their actions the closest thing to a crusade that their generation had seen.[2] Although a great many British wanted intervention on the side of the Loyalists, the majority were also sympathetic to their cause but content with Non-Intervention, while only a very small minority actually went to Spain.

In spite of the intention (stated January 9th, 1937) to apply the Foreign Enlistment Act to Spain, the British Government found enforcement extremely difficult. Neither the extension of Non-Intervention to prohibit volunteers, nor the declaration that British passports were, unless specifically stated, invalid for Spain, had much effect by themselves in preventing the departure of manpower. Enlistment, which previously was conducted in the open although taxed with new difficulties, still continued. The British authorities of course knew that many young men going to Paris as tourists had other intentions but they could do very little (one could even travel without a passport by simply stating the trip to Paris was only for the weekend.)

---

[1] *Times*, December 10, 1937.
[2] Garrett, *Mussolini's Roman Empire*, p. 183.

Once in France, if found medically, and more important, politically acceptable, enlistees were helped to reach Spain. The principal organization behind recruitment was the British Communist Party, which symbolized for many the only group willing to translate the struggle of Democracy against Fascism into action. People who had distrusted the Party in the past now became party recruits. The Communists facilitated everything. They organized special aid projects, showed propagandist films and held mass meetings. Monetary support was often found among sections of the population least able to afford it; financial appeals produced anything from wedding rings, to shabby heirlooms, to unopened pay checks. Like a revival meeting, converts came forth. Those eager for service in Spain would be referred to proper channels. Much of the instinctive hostility towards Franco which exists in England today has been traced to these Communist campaigns.

The British volunteers were generally like any men that seek a mass movement. They craved an outward discipline through which their lives could have meaning; they found conditions at home intolerable and they saw the Communist Party as a hope and a guide. Most were from the working class, practically all unemployed. Of those with party affiliations, more often than not they were Communist. There were intellectuals; students from English universities, young writers, and disillusioned pacifists. There were adventurers. Most were in their twenties or early thirties, but age could extend anywhere from sixteen to fifty six! The early volunteers had usually been exposed to some sort of military experience; later the reverse was true. Most were inspired by their mission. "I go forward," said one, "confident that I shall do my duty against the enemies of progress, and that whatever comes, the strength of the workers will overcome all opposition in Spain and the rest of the world." [1] But idealism was not the only explanation for their actions. The die-hard Communists used Spain as a training ground to practice the art of insurrection which one day could be applied at home.[2] Their cause needed martyrs. "It was tragic," said Attlee, "that all the time the Communists were intriguing and seeking to divert the contest into a battle for Communism." [3] In the beginning the Communist Party sent members to fight; most of these, along with a handful of students, were killed. Casualties were indeed so high that recruiting of Party members was

---

[1] Rust, p. 21.
[2] Hyde, p. 59.
[3] Attlee, p. 94.

discouraged, and new volunteers had to be "non-Communists whose deaths would assist the immediate aims of the Party without jeopardizing the coming struggle for power at home." [1]

A British Battalion came into existence on December 27, 1936 at Madriqueras.[2] The organizational structure of the British Battalion, like the other International contingents, followed Communist practice, having political commissars who countersigned all military orders. Before, owing to their insufficient numbers, British soldiers were scattered among other battalions, principally German and French. In the defense of Madrid there had been only thirty British. Due to insufficient training and lack of manpower, the British Battalion when formed did not see major action until the battle of Jarama in February 1937. Included as part of the XV International Brigade, they were given the task of stopping the Rebel threat to cut the main Madrid-Valencia road. The battle began on February 12 and continued through the rest of the month. The price of victory to the British Battalion was catastrophic. Over half the original number were lost in either dead, wounded or captured. In the ensuing months casualties continued to mount, so by the fall of 1937, in spite of new arrivals, only several dozen Britons were left at the front, although later enlistments brought the battalion back to full strength. Unquestionably brave, their propaganda value was more important than military prudence. Left defending positions too long or ordered to attack too soon, they fought as shock troops in the greatest battles, usually in forward posts. Heavy reliance on the International Brigades, continuing until they were withdrawn, kept the high casualty rate of the British Battalion fairly constant. Of approximately 2,000 English who went to Spain 432 were known as killed in action, but many more reported missing were assumed dead. In addition to the slain, there were roughly 1,203 other casualties, of which many had recovered to fight again but at least 495 were sent home before the League of Nations withdrawals.[3] For the relief of the men and their dependants there had been organized the Wounded and Dependants Aid Committee, which had collected £45,574. To meet increased financial responsibilities, imposed by the final evacuation, a nationwide drive was organized supported by such

---

[1] Hyde, p. 60.

[2] There is some dispute about how many Britons composed this first battalion. Rust estimates the numbers at nearly five hundred (*Britons in Spain*, p. 25) while its Captain, Wintringham puts it at a bit more than one hundred an fifty, divided into weak companies. (*English Captain*, p. 91.)

[3] *Times*, October 13, 1938.

men as the Dean of Chester, J. B. Priestley, Sidney Webb and Clement Attlee.

But in spite of their sacrifice all crusaders should be treated with skepticism; sacrifice and heroic devotion for a cause are generally cloaks for personal frustration, hatred, pride or desire for revenge. These qualities have always existed in people, but it was the opportunity to consecrate their efforts to a mission abroad when none existed at home which made the International Brigade possible and made it a phenomenon of the times.

* *
*

Despite their differences Chamberlain made no move to replace Eden with a man more attuned to this own ideas. Instead, he preferred to circumvent the Foreign Office through extra diplomatic channels. The most active of Chamberlain's go-betweens was Sir Horace Wilson, a civil servant, who normally advised the Government on industrial affairs. Chamberlain's contacts with the Italian Ambassador early in 1938 were made by employing Sir Joseph Ball, the director of the Conservative Party Research Department.[1] In addition, the Prime Minister also made use of Lady Chamberlain, the wife of his late half-brother Austen, who was in Rome at the time. Ciano was also using Lady Chamberlain to advance his own negotiations; she was treated politely but regarded as somewhat of a fool. On her wearing the Fascist Party badge, Ciano commented that he was too patriotic to appreciate such a gesture on the part of an Englishwoman.[2]

Chamberlain sought the advice of those who agreed with his policy. The British Ambassador in Rome Sir Eric Drummond, since the death of his brother the Earl of Perth, wholeheartedly in favour of appeasement, was very anxious to promote a rapprochement with Mussolini. (In Germany, Ambassador Sir Eric Phipps, very anti-Hitler, was replaced in 1937 by the docile Sir Nevile Henderson. A further casualty of Chamberlain's policy was the Permanent Under Secretary of Foreign Affairs, Sir Robert Vansittart who in December 1937 was "promoted" to the ineffectual post of Chief Diplomatic Advisor to the Foreign Secretary.)

During January (1938) the problem of Anglo-Italian conversations was left unsettled, neither Chamberlain nor Eden wishing to push their

---

[1] Hoare writes matter-of-factly about Chamberlain's outside contacts, *Nine Troubled Years*, p. 278, but Duff Cooper does not regard them so routine, *Old Men Forget*, p. 214.

[2] Ciano, *Journal Politique*, pp. 85–86, 101.

respective points of view. On January 25, in Paris, Eden found the
French attitude coincided with his own: the Spanish problem had to be
included in any general settlement.[1] (Conversations with the French
had also been held, between Chamberlain, Halifax, Eden, Chautemps
and Delbos during the previous November when Chamberlain persuaded the French that Mussolini be approached before Hitler.) [2] But
French support, although reassuring, was not sufficient to impress
Chamberlain, who, in writing a letter to his sister-in-law enclosed an
important message for Mussolini. Shown to the Italian Dictator on
February 1, the correspondence expressed the desire for conversations
at the end of February, adding that Great Britain was preparing herself
for the formal recognition of the Italian Empire. Mussolini, wholeheartedly approving, told Lady Chamberlain to reply that he had
every intention to find with Britain a common accord, which would
endure as a basis of cooperation.[3]

On the same day the sinking of the British ship *Endymion* off Cartagena provoked a meeting of Ambassadors of the countries involved in
the Nyon Patrol Scheme. Eden was brief; confining himself strictly
to the matter at hand he informed the delegates (French and Italian)
that due to this latest act of piracy Britain was now reserving the
right to "destroy every submerged submarine encountered in the part
of the Western Mediterranean reserved for the British patrol ships." [4]
The Italians, to avoid suspicion, had no choice but to acquiesce. On
February 4, Eden, the shipping attack still fresh in his mind, reaffirmed
"that in the British view there can be no general solution of Mediterranean problems which would exclude Spain from its scope and that
therefore a definite understanding with regard to Italy's intentions in
that country should be a necessary preliminary to any Anglo-Italian
rapprochement." [5] On February 10th Grandi said that Italy was ready
to discuss formally its differences with Britain; Eden treated the offer
cavalierly. Two days later, in Birmingham, he said:

> If we are to have peace in your time it means that in any agreements we make
> today there must be no sacrifice of principles and no shirking of responsibilities
> merely to obtain quick results that may not be permanent ... We offer friendship
> to all, but on equal terms. For it is not by seeking to buy temporary good will
> that peace is made, but on a basis of frank reciprocity with mutual respect.[6]

[1] Churchill, p. 199.
[2] Feiling, p. 334.
[3] Ciano, *Journal Politique*, p. 117.
[4] *GD.*, p. 578.
[5] *USD.*, 1938, I, p. 135.
[6] Eden, p. 252.

Italy's tactics to let matters drift were suddenly changed during the next few days by German threats towards the independence of Austria. In a secret message February 16th, Ciano instructed Grandi to speed up preliminary arrangements because, if

the Anschluss be an accomplished fact, should Greater Germany by then press on our frontier with the weight of its whole seventy million, then it would become increasingly difficult for us to reach an agreement or even talk with the English, since it would be impossible to prevent the entire world interpreting our policy of rapprochement with London as a journey to Canossa under German pressure.[1]

The Austrian crisis also had effect in Britain; on February 16 and again the following day Eden invited Grandi to the Foreign Office. The Italian Ambassador put him off, explaining that he was awaiting new instructions, and the second time that he was going to play golf. ("I hate golf but pretend to play it when necessary ") In the meantime Sir Joseph Ball, Chamberlain's confidential agent, in contact almost daily with Grandi since January 15th, called at the Italian Embassy to convince the Ambassador to change his mind; he pointed out "it was very probable that the Prime Minister, Mr. Chamberlain, would himself take part in the conversation." [2] Grandi outlined the reasons why he had avoided meeting Eden, ("I simply could not lend myself ... to anything which might possibly be exploited, in England or abroad as a maneuver against the Rome-Berlin Axis."), but said if the Prime Minister were willing to have personal contact with him he would be available at any time. Ball contacted Chamberlain at once. That evening an invitation was telephoned to the Italian Embassy inviting Grandi to Downing Steet at 11:30 A.M. the next day.

Chamberlain began by expressing concern over Austria. Having heard, through Lord Perth, about Ciano's letter, which fortuitously for Italy was not delivered until the morning of February 18th, he asked if Grandi had received these instructions, could he reveal their contents. Grandi was evasive; not only did he refuse to make any formal communication but he steadfastly refused to discuss the Austrian situation, except to say that there had not been any prior agreement between Hitler and Mussolini, but he cleverly threatened a future agreement if Britain did not settle her differences with Fascist Italy. Chamberlain, impressed, glanced at Eden and asked Grandi what

[1] *Ciano's Diplomatic Papers*, p. 162.
[2] *Ibid.*, pp. 165–166. According to Feiling, Chamberlain had the view that the Foreign Office was trying to prevent his seeing Grandi. Feiling, p. 337.

practical suggestions he could give to bring about positive results between their countries. Grandi answered that they should immediately "without prejudicial conditions" begin official conversations. Eden, silent up to now, interrupted sharply; finding the Italian attitude extremely vague, he accused Grandi of pretending to ignore the whole question of Spain,

which is of fundamental importance to Anglo-Italian relations and prejudicial to them. What is the use of official conversations in Rome and London, if they are not preceeded by a precise agreement and if a satisfactory solution of the Spanish question has not been reached? In January 1937 an agreement was reached between England and Italy, which has shown itself in practice to be sterile and useless, solely because the Spanish question was merely touched upon in that agreement, and not discussed and settled so as to avoid the possibility of its constituting, in the future, the source of possible friction and disagreement between the two countries. To declare open official conversations between Rome and London without previous agreement on the Spanish question, means giving rise to dangerous illusions and exaggerated prospects of the course of the Anglo-Italian negotiations.[1]

Afraid that a British concession on Abyssinia would not be reciprocated by any corresponding Italian undertaking, in a review of Anglo-Italian relations since the Gentleman's Agreement, Eden insisted it was necessary to create a situation whereby "unfortunate coincidences" would not reoccur. While Chamberlain accepted Grandi's proposition that Italian-British discussions would result in favourable consequences, Eden was unimpressed.

When the conversations resumed after lunch, Eden and Chamberlain were no nearer agreement than before. Chamberlain was determined to go ahead with talks and he used Grandi to enforce his position against his own Foreign Secretary. As Grandi described the scene,

Chamberlain and Eden were not a Prime Minister and a Foreign Minister discussing with the Ambassador of a Foreign Power a delicate situation of an international character. They were ... two enemies confronting each other, like cocks in true fighting posture. The questions and queries addressed to me by Chamberlain were all, without exception, intentionally put with the aim of producing replies which would have the effect of contradicting and overthrowing the basis or argument on which Eden had evidently previously constructed, or by which he had attempted to justify, his miserable anti-Italian and anti-Fascist policy in opposition to Chamberlain and before his colleagues in the Cabinet.[2]

[1] *Ciano's Diplomatic Papers*, p. 172.
[2] *Ibid.*, pp. 182–183. (Samuel Hoare felt that this account was too exaggerated to be true. However, outside of general observations on Grandi's character, Hoare gives no source for his beliefs. *Nine Troubled Years*, p. 279).

Chamberlain said he was unable to give a definite reply until after a Cabinet meeting; by the following Monday he hoped that Grandi would also have confirmation from his own government. To make sure he clearly understood Chamberlain's intention, Grandi asked if he were right in assuming the talks would then begin immediately, without waiting for the consequences of the British proposal before the Non-Intervention Committee. Chamberlain replied that this interpretation was correct. Grandi then insisted the conference take place in Rome. Chamberlain held that London, in view of the conversations recently in progress at the Foreign Office, was more practical and logical. Eden was more emphatic; he considered it absolutely necessary that the talks – "if they do actually take place and when they take place" – be held in the British capital, because

it is in London that the discussions of the Non-Intervention Committee are held and continue to be held, and it was evident that any Anglo-Italian conversations which might take place would have to keep in step with the work of the Non-Intervention Committee.[1]

Out of a sincere but questionable belief that the place of the negotiations would favourably influence their results, Chamberlain finally conceded to Italy.

Throughout this interview Chamberlain no doubt gave Grandi the impression that he was thoroughly resigned to Italian intervention. Believing sincerely in an agreement with Britain, Grandi would not have jeopardized his position had he suspected that the British Prime Minister would regard his attacks on Non-Intervention with hostility.[2] But Chamberlain, though he could tolerate Italian violations, was unable to purge their bitter presence from his future negotiations.

2. THE RESIGNATION OF EDEN

Eden came to the Cabinet meeting on February 19th already decided on resignation. Four days previously the American *Chargé d'Affairs* Johnson revealed that he was aware of the cleavage that existed between Chamberlain and his Foreign Secretary. He claimed that an informant told him that Eden had sent in his resignation 10 days earlier, "that it caused a good deal of excitement and considerable pressure

---

[1] *Ibid.*, p. 180.
[2] Grandi "is dying from desire for a rapprochement with London, and hates the Germans," wrote Ciano, *Journal Politique*, p. 122.

was brought upon him to withdraw it." [1] The Foreign Minister's decision however came as a "surprise and shock to his Cabinet colleagues," [2] who tried to get him to change his mind. Eden was unmoved; it was plain to him that Chamberlain wanted to be Foreign Secretary as well as Prime Minister and he refused to be a stooge to a policy with which he so violently disagreed. Although Chamberlain was backed unanimously by his Cabinet, he nevertheless, realizing the situation's seriousness, proposed adjournment until the following day. In conversations during the interval Eden told Chamberlain that the Italian Government should have made a positive gesture, such as their acceptance of the British plan for withdrawal, before entering negotiations. When the Prime Minister asked if acceptance of such a formula would make any difference, Eden admitted "quite straightforwardly and simply that it would not. He had other objections which would still remain." [3] (In addition to the question of Italian negotiations and Spain, Eden was miffed at Chamberlain's failure to pursue, or to inform him about, an offer for closer diplomatic ties made by the United States the middle of January ,1938.) A Sunday meeting was a rare occurrence and when the ministers assembled that afternoon there was a large restive crowd, sympathetic to Eden, milling around 10 Downing Street. Chamberlain stated that he had received private assurances from Grandi that Mussolini would accept the British formula regarding withdrawal of volunteers. As revealed by Chamberlain in the Commons, February 21, 1938, the communication said: "The Italian Ambassador informs the Prime Minister that he has submitted to the Italian Government the proposals suggested at their meeting last Friday, and is glad to convey to him the acceptance by the Italian Government of the British formula concerning the withdrawal of foreign volunteers and granting of belligerent rights." Eden was adamant; Chamberlain accepted his resignation. As he left the meeting on the way to settle his affairs at the Foreign Office, he was greeted by the crowd with loud cheers. Duff Cooper said, "This, I am afraid, will stiffen his attitude, because he will feel that he has popular opinion behind him, which indeed he has." [4]

Eden had been associated in the public eye as the defender of the principles of the Covenant, and his resignation seemed to admit that the British Government was no longer interested in their enforcement.

[1] *USD.*, 1938, I, p. 137.
[2] Hoare, *Nine Troubled Years*, pp. 279. See also: Cooper, pp. 211–212, and Minney, p. 101.
[3] *Hansard*, 332, col. 258.
[4] Cooper, p. 213.

The weekend Cabinet meetings had caused widespread interest and although supported by the Cabinet, Chamberlain was put in the awkward position of justifying himself with his own party as well as with the Opposition. The Labour Party introduced a general motion of censure. "It looks rather curious to us," said Attlee, "that just when a colleague is being attacked by people overseas, by foreign countries, when week after week, he is abused in every possible way, his colleagues do not stand by him... The last occasion when anything of this kind happened was in 1905, when the German Government dictated the dismissal of M. Delcassé." [1] Churchill said that Italian attacks on Eden amounted to a demand that unless the Foreign Secretary went there would be no progress in Anglo-Italian talks.[2] Throughout most of the debates during this period one can not help being struck by the presence of a certain insincerity. When the Civil War raised the problem of protection of British shipping, the Labour Party became immediately the protectors of British prestige; the Eden crisis was similarly exploited, the former Foreign Secretary being treated as a sort of martyr to the cause of resolute policy. If Eden had been temperamentally so inclined, he might have been more embarrassing to the Government; but his speech on February 21st in the Commons, although made with sincerity, created an impression that "there was really no issue for resignation, unless he objected fundamentally to enter into any conversations with so untrustworthy a person as Mussolini." [3] Eden concluded his personal explanation (Grandi was listening in the Gallery) by saying:

I do not believe that we can make progress in European appeasement, more particularly in the light of the events of the past few days ... if we allow the impression to gain currency abroad that we yield to constant pressure. I am certain in my own mind that progress depends above all on the temper of the nation, and that temper must find expression in a firm spirit. That spirit, I am confident, is there; not to give voice to it is, I believe, fair neither to this country nor to the world.

The extremely hostile Opposition booed Simon when he answered for the Foreign Office at Question Time; when Chamberlain spoke, they listened in silence; on one occasion when he said,

It has always seemed to me that in dealing with foreign countries we do not give ourselves a chance of success unless we try to understand their mentality,

---

[1] *Hansard*, 333, col. 67.

[2] *Ibid.*, 239; see also Lloyd George's remarks, *Ibid.*, 260. The French *Chargé d'Affaires* in Rome, Blondel, believed that Grandi got Eden's direct dismissal. He described the Foreign Minister as an "espèce de Pitt ressuscité contre le Napoléon Italien." Blondel, p. 378.

[3] Amery, p. 234.

which is not always the same as our own, and it really is astonishing to contemplate how the identically same facts are regarded from two different angles. I am informed from many sources that all this time when to us it appeared that the obstacles to conversations had arisen entirely by Italian action, exactly the opposite view was being held in Rome.

they laughed. They were sober when he said,

the League as constitutued today is unable to provide collective security for anybody, then I say we must not try to delude small weak nations into thinking that they will be protected by the League against aggression and acting accordingly, when we know that nothing of the kind can be expected.

From then on collective security, used as a catch-all for many Labour policies and a substitute for Non-Intervention, took precedence, and practically all the speeches from their benches that afternoon concentrated more on the surrender of Covenant principles than Eden's resignation. Their motion of censure was of course defeated (330 to 168) but the relatively large number of ministral abstentions (25) testified to the restlessness which existed in the Government. The most prominent Conservative to support Eden was Winston Churchill but the only one to follow him in resignation was the Under-Secretary, Lord Cranborn.

Eden left the Government at a fortunate time. Most of the stigmata which was later attached to Chamberlain and his clique resulted from the appeasement of Germany, not Spanish policy. At the time of his resignation Eden was disgusted with an ineffective policy of Non-Intervention, but the policy had been engineered by Eden and it is hard to see how he can be disassociated from its unpleasant implications.

CHAPTER VIII

NEGOTIATING WITH MUSSOLINI

I. LORD HALIFAX BECOMES FOREIGN MINISTER

Eden's obvious successor was Lord Halifax. Close to Chamberlain
in both temperament and age, Halifax had already worked with Chamberlain, on one famous occasion he was his personal representative to
Germany, and he strongly shared the Prime Minister's views on foreign
policy. Although there was no doubt of Halifax's qualifications, it was
probably the dislike of his politics, so closely identical with those of
his boss, which prompted Attlee to challenge the appointment in the
Commons.[1] With Halifax's accession came, if not started before, a
decided drift from Spanish affairs which, outside of a general desire to
ignore the war as much as possible, and the attitude of the new Foreign
Secretary himself, was precipitated mostly by Hitler's activities in
Eastern Europe.

Meanwhile, there was still Mussolini to consider, and with Eden
out of the way conversations could begin. On February 22 Lord Perth
was called to London for instructions. Before departure Perth asked
Ciano whether he had any suggestions to make for the coming conversations. Ciano agreed that the subjects would be those with which
they were already familiar, but cynically dismissed

some which had in the meantime lapsed, such as the problem of the Balearics,
and others, such as the problem of Spain, which had been transferred to another
body. Naturally, on the Italian side, the question of legal recognition of the
empire was being added.[2]

The same day Ciano expressed his dissatisfaction with the way
Franco was conducting the war; impatiently he wrote,

---

[1] Halifax was appointed February 26; the debate on his appointment took place two days
later.
[2] *Ciano's Diplomatic Papers*, p. 187.

Fortune is not a train which passes every day at the same time nor an honest woman who gives herself for life. She is a prostitute who offers herself fleetingly and then passes on to others. If you can't manage to seize her by the hair you lose her.[1]

But the prospects of victory were sufficiently promising that it was unnecessary to displease Chamberlain by either altering the present situation by "sending fresh reinforcements to Spain or by failing to implement the arrangements contemplated by the British formula." [2]

Lord Perth returned to Rome March 6th, opening conversations with Ciano two days later. In order that talks begin in an atmosphere of good feeling Perth presented Ciano with a personal message from Halifax who expressed his desire for the rebirth of the old friendship which had traditionally existed between their countries. Perth said that Halifax had addressed an appeal to the British press (not, of course, the Opposition's) to avoid anti-Italian campaigns, but warned that "the problem to which British public opinion attaches the most importance is that of the evacuation of volunteers from Spain. It would therefore be necessary to achieve concrete progress on this subject as soon as possible." [3] Lord Perth suggested that an Italian evacuation of the Balearic Islands would constitute a gesture "certain to arouse a most widespread and favourable response among the British public" [4] Ciano calmly replied that this last request was strange since it was well known that in the Balearics there were no Italian landforces. Lord Perth did not press the point, but he might well have; Majorca all through the war resembled an Italian colony. Certain streets were given Roman names; the harbour became a naval station; the airfields served as a base for innumerable Italian bombing raids. After the war Mussolini wanted Franco to grant him military leases. Lord Perth's preliminary remarks were indicative of the concern with which the British Government continually regarded the question of the Balearics. The British agenda emphasized the paragraphs relative to Spain, the question of Ethiopia, and the *status quo* in the Mediterranean. Ciano's reservations made it obvious that Italy was trying to create as many loopholes as possible; he objected to Perth's statement that the Abyssinian question would only be handled after concrete

---

[1] Ciano, *Journal Politique*, p. 133.

[2] In Chamberlain's speech, *Hansard*, 322, cols. 62–63; the Prime Minister also said that a settlement of the Spanish Question had to be an essential feature of any agreement; and if such an accord were concluded Britain would solicit the League to recognize Mussolini's rights in Ethopia.

[3] *Ciano's Diplomatic Papers*, p. 188.

[4] *Ibid.*

progress had been made on the evacuation of volunteers, claiming that this constituted a distinct change over the previous position, which had merely requested acceptance of the British formula. Asking for clarification of the terms "concrete progress," he wanted to know "what the British Government intended to do if a certain period of time elapsed between a possible agreement between the two Governments on the various points submitted for [their] examination and the solution of the Spanish problem," [1] and also when Britain intended to bring the question of Ethiopian recognition before the League. Perth replied that Britain intended to raise the question at the Council meeting in May,[2] but suggested postponing until further conversations the other points: the Spanish Question and the formulation of a general Mediterranean Pact. The most embarrassing issues, therefore, were saved for last, and when discussed, judging from later impressions, were inconclusively handled. By his unconscious habit of always giving Italy the benefit of any doubt, of making allowances, in this case, for Italy's difficulty to unilaterally withdraw from Spain, Perth put himself at a disadvantage; convinced that Mussolini was sincere he told the American Ambassador that it would not be fair "to let the negotiations drop merely because Moscow may be the stumbling block in the plan for a more general withdrawal of volunteers." [3]

Throughout March Labour hammered away at the Government's failure to protect British interests from armed intervention. At Question Time they made constant reference to Italian breaches of Non-Intervention since beginning conversations, enforcing their allegations by repeated quotation of the daily press. In a Foreign Office memorandum dated March 15th, Lord Halifax wrote that because they had connected the Italian conversations with a settlement of the Spanish issue, the British Government was "particularly anxious to make progress with the work of the Non-Intervention Committee" in order to test "by actual performance the value of Italian assurances." [4] The Italian bombing of Barcelona on March 18th created a public sensation. Acting on Foreign Office directives, Lord Perth gave Ciano an *aide-mémoire* which said that "in view of British public opinion it would be difficult in case of repetition of such attacks to bring the negotiations to a successful conclusion." [5] Lord Perth,

[1] *Ibid.*, p. 191.
[2] *Ibid.*
[3] *USD.*, 1938, I, p. 143.
[4] *BD.*, I, p. 53.
[5] *GD.*, p. 622.

personally transmitting the note, emphasized the delicate situation which would be created for Chamberlain unless the attacks were stopped. Although Ciano claimed that the attacks did not originate with Italy (in reality they had been personally ordered by Mussolini who thereby displeased Franco), he promised to do something about them.

As the Government became more intent on an agreement with Mussolini, the British public demanded stronger action to stop his intervention. Their diversity of opinion was more reflected in the British press than in the Parliamentary parties. On the extreme Right, completely lacking in integrity, was the chain of papers (*Daily Mail, Evening News, Sunday Dispatch*, and *Daily Dispatch*) owned by Lord Rothermere. Lurid with Republican atrocities – prisoners cruci-fied, nuns raped, eyes gouged – the Rothermere press not only printed the news which suited its own purpose, but made a regular practice of publishing outright fabrications – Rothermere justified his later sup-port for Non-Intervention by its contribution to Franco's victory. Also showing unqualified support for Franco were the Catholic Weeklies (*Catholic Herald, Catholic Times, Universe*) which, taking their general direction from the sympathies of the Vatican, showed considerable irresponsibility at news reporting. Although also to the Right in editorial policy, *The Observer* was more scrupulous with facts. Some papers started the war moderately rightist, pro-Franco, but as the war progressed they moved moved towards the center. Such newspapers were the *Daily Telegraph* and the *Daily Express* of Lord Beaverbrook, who became surprisingly impartial by denouncing both sides.

Among papers more or less in the Center were the *Times* and the *Manchester Guardian*. But as with the newspapers of the Right as well as those of the Left there was a division within a division. The *Times* supported the Conservative position while the *Guardian* criticized the policy of Non-Intervention and showed sympathy for the Spanish Republic. Both papers though were highly impartial when it came to news coverage. On the Left, the *Daily Herald*, published by Trans-port House, naturally supported the Labour position, while the Liberal *News Chronicle*, not attached to any official organization, afforded to be more independent. At the extreme Left the *Daily Worker* slavishly reflected the policy of Moscow. The editorial policy among provincial newspapers was mostly pro-Government. This situation was somewhat due to the extent of amalgamation which existed among the press in that area. The largest chain of papers of this nature was that controlled by the Kemsley Press. Created Baron for his services to the Conservative Party, Lord Kemsley managed the principal papers in many larger provincial cities, like Aberdeen and Newcastle. In addition he controlled a wide assortment of smaller, but collectively important, evening papers, located mostly in the North. In London, his empire extended to the important *Sunday Times*, the *Sunday Graphic*, and the *Daily Sketch*. Sir Harold Mitchell, one time Vice-Chairman of the Conservative Party, estimated the combined worth of these papers over twenty times more important than the *Manchester Guardian*. Singly one of the strongest provincial papers, probably the most significant outside of the *Guardian*, was the *Yorkshire Post*. Independent, but with strong traditional links to the Conservative Party, the *Post* was a big city daily with wide rural readership. Thousands of readers could undoubtedly confirm that the *Post* had been present in the daily life of their family for the past two generations. Widely circulated, its general appeal made it basically as much a part of the region as Yorkshire pudding. The *Post* rigourously separated news from their editorial policy, which was strongly in favour of Non-Intervention. In this respect they created as well as reflected their readers' opinions (that they could also go against mass feeling and the Conservative policy was demonstrated by their opposition to the Munich agreement), but as the provinces are generally more cautious than London, it was probably more a simultanous identity than apparently either. Except, however, for the newspapers on the extremes no British journal called outwardly for intervention, and most of them would have been most satisfied with an effective policy of Non-Intervention.

Meanwhile, on April 11th, still trying to discredit the Anglo-Italian negotiations, Arthur Henderson presented the Commons with strong evidence that Italy was undermining the talks by continuing intervention. He challenged the Government,

to be frank with the House, and to cease to hide behind [the] barricade of official ignorance. I hesitate to charge the Government with deliberate dishonesty, but their attitude is due either to gross inefficiency or to a deliberate intention to mislead the public... I ask the Government to give the facts, so that the public may realize upon whom should be placed the real responsibility for the tragedy now being enacted in Spain.

R. A. Butler replied that it was difficult to authenticate reports coming from Spain, but nevertheless the Spanish situation according to their information had not been materially "altered." The Government, determined to let nothing interfere with their negotiations, created a sense of urgency which gave Ciano the impression that Chamberlain had staked his and the whole political future of the Conservative Party on an agreement with Italy.[1]

During the course of the talks Chamberlain remained optimistic; at the Easter recess of Commons he made a speech (at Birmingham) in which he said:

> During the recent weeks we have been engaging in conversations with ... the Italian Government, with the result that a whole cloud of suspicions and misunderstandings has been blown away. There is today a good prospect of restoring those old friendly relations which, until they were recently broken, had lasted so long that they had become almost traditional between our two countries.[2]

Once the agreement is published, he said, if you are not of the same opinion and think I have been fooled then "I will be prepared to eat my hat." Although he referred to the ancient Greeks, he made no mention of Spain.

The Agreements and Declarations, signed in Rome by Count Ciano and Lord Perth on April 16th, consisted of a series of eight separate and self-contained instruments,[3] including, most importantly, the Italian assurances on Spanish policy. In three short paragraphs Ciano reaffirmed the Italian intention to adhere to and apply the British evacuation formula, as soon as conditions were determined by the Non-Intervention Committee. He pledged if this evacuation were not completed while the war was being waged the remaining troops would leave as soon as it were over, stating that the

> Italian Government have no territorial or political aims, and seek no privileged economic position, in or with regard to either metropolitan Spain, the Balearic Islands, any of Spanish possessions overseas, or the Spanish zone of Morocco, and that they have no intention whatever of keeping any armed forces in any of the said territories.[4]

While acknowledging these assurances Lord Perth wrote that he hardly need remind Ciano that the entry into force of the agreement was contingent upon a settlement of the Spanish Question which would then be followed by a British recognition of Italian sovereignty over Ethiopia.

[1] Ciano, *Journal Politique*, p. 142.
[2] Chamberlain, p. 171.
[3] *Cmd.* 5726.
[4] *Ibid.*

Reaction to the agreement was generally favourable. The newspapers of the Right shared the enthusiasm of Chamberlain; those on the Left, like Labour's *Daily Herald*, were critical. Several days before, the *Manchester Guardian* had accurately written:

> There is some criticism of the agreement here on the grounds that every real difficulty has been passed over. That is to say, wherever British and Italian interests are in direct and tangible contradiction... no settlement has been attempted. In other words, the impending agreement may remove the misunderstandings that exist between the two powers but it does not remove any of the tangible causes of conflict.[1]

In diplomatic correspondence one has to consider what has not been said as much as what has, what was inferred as much as what was not; the terms of a treaty are like classical verse: there are precise reasons for the insertion of every word and phrase. Applying this criterion to the Anglo-Italian agreement, it is clear that Britain did not anticipate the Spanish war to last much longer. The treaty reflects Chamberlain's desire for an instrument which would serve as a basis for negotiations of future agreements over the Mediterranean and Near East, and it was not imagined that the Spanish Codicil (given a priority incommensurate with desire because of public opinion) would become a later hindrance. The treaty was signed at a time when Franco's success in Aragon seemed to portend his imminent victory, (on April 15th, the day before the signing, the capture of Vinaroz had cut the Republic in two). Ciano's expectation that Italian troops would be in Spain at the end of the war, followed by a strong enunciation of Spanish political and territorial claims, clearly suggests the real *quid pro quo*: British acquiescence of Italian troops in Spain until the end of the war in exchange for a firm statement "volunteers" would be withdrawn as soon as it was over. (The Republic's London Ambassador, Pablo Azcarate, interpreting the treaty in this light, sent a strong protest denouncing the British acceptance of Italian troops while at the same time seeming to work for their withdrawal through Non-Intervention; he wrote that the shame and indignation caused by this policy made the Republic keep their relations with Britain to a minimum.) [2] Furthermore, latitude in interpreting the words "settlement of the Spanish Question" was suspiciously evasive; while Chamberlain believed the Italian Government would keep their promises in spirit as well as in letter, Labour wanted a more precise definition. When the

---

[1] *Guardian*, April 10, 1938.
[2] Thomas, p. 531.

point was pressed, Chamberlain was vague. In the Commons on May 2 he said,

it would be wrong to try to define the circumstances in which one could say that a settlement had been arrived at. It may be that later on we shall get nearer the time when we can give a definition.

Attlee retorted that Chamberlain was

asking the House to approve a Treaty that is to come into force on the specific terms that there should be a settlement in Spain, and now he says that he cannot tell the House what a settlement is. It is ridiculous.

Intentional ambiguities of this sort made the Anglo-Italian treaty a preparation for burial (the corpse being the issue of Spain); however, the tendency of Labour to protest frequently proved embarrassing to Conservative pallbearers too intent on their task.

2. BRINGING THE TREATY INTO FORCE

For a brief period improvement of relations justified Chamberlain's initial optimism, and Britain, true to her promise, removed League hindrance to recognition of the Italian Empire. At the Council meeting May 12 the question of whether Italy's position in Ethiopia be left to the judgment of individual members was discussed and subsequently approved, over warnings from the Emperor Haile Selassie that this implied the end of the League. On May 12 a plea by Alvarez Del Vayo to have the Council implement the Assembly's pledge of October 2, 1937 [1] was rejected by a vote of four to two, with eight abstentions. That more delegations abstained than voted was due to a rather crude procedural maneuver which, allowing only two hours for consideration of the resolution, did not give the delegates sufficient time to consult their home governments. It probably made little difference. Lord Halifax's speech had clearly intimated that the League had no more business being involved in the question of the Civil War.

Mussolini gave no evidence that he appreciated British efforts. When the French tried to follow the British accord with their own – a step welcomed by Britain, who throughout her talks with Italy had repeatedly suggested France be included (On April 28th and 29th Chamberlain and Halifax had promised France not to put their accord

---

[1] i.e. to consider ending the policy of Non-Intervention, if complete withdrawal of non-Spanish combatants could not be obtained in the "near future."

with Italy into effect before the end of the Franco-Italian conversations) [1] – the Duce showed more hostility than enthusiasm, having no desire to foster better relations with an ally of Britain. On May 15 in Genoa he shattered all hopes of a rapprochement with France while pledging to support the agreement with Britain. Mussolini delivered his speech from a rostrum at the end of an aisle of sixteen statues representing Fascist Italy's military victories, five of which were in Spain. "You will allow me to be circumspect about our conversations with France, since they are still in progress," he said, "I do now know if they will reach a conclusion, because in one extremely vital matter, the war in Spain, we stand on opposite sides of the barricade." [2] Mussolini was instinctively more anti-French than anti-British; he thought the French a people ruined by alcohol, syphilis, and journalism.[3] Trying to obtain the conclusion of the treaty with Britain before any fulfillment of the Spanish proviso, Mussolini's speech gave the British a new cause for concern and did nothing to advance his prospects. On May 18th, Lord Perth informed Ciano that in view of the action taken in Geneva to remove obstacles to the recognition of the Italian Empire, the Government was disappointed Mussolini should have expressed himself so negatively. Perth said it should not be forgotten that "Chamberlain has encountered very serious parliamentary difficulties in order to bring about the agreement with Italy and that even today the opposition has not been disbanded"; [4] the Prime Minister, anxious to vindicate claims that his policy would effectively reduce European tensions, saw nothing in Mussolini's attitude nor in his conduct of the war which was reassuring. Mussolini's tactics did not appear too far sighted. Perhaps he was testing Britain's connections with France, but more likely he overjudged the island mentality of the British and failed to appreciate the concern they had over his hostility towards France. It was quite hopeless to expect him to understand the role of public opinion in a democracy, but he was smart enough though to realize that he had gone too far in his Genoa talk.

On June 2nd, Ciano gave a speech at Milan which praised the efforts being made by Chamberlain and Halifax to clear away "the rubble of the past." The next day Perth came to Ciano's office to thank him; he also asked that Ciano use his influence with Franco to stop the indiscriminate bombing attacks which were outraging the

[1] Bonnet, *De Washington au Quai D'Orsay*, p. 110.
[2] *Times*, May 16, 1938.
[3] Ciano, *Journal Politique*, p. 184.
[4] *Ciano's Diplomatic Papers*, p. 207.

British public. Ciano promised to see what he could do, and, deciding to profit from the bliss created by his Milan discourse, asked Perth straightaway for the finalization of the April 16th agreements; he claimed that Italy had done everything in her power to completely fulfill her pledges and said that any delay on Britain's part would only diminish their final value. Chamberlain, Perth replied, was also eager to bring the accords into effect, but "naturally, as far as Spain is concerned, he must have a sound reason for declaring that the problem is moving towards a final solution." [1]

Bombardments meanwhile continued and were repeatedly directed against neutral British shipping. Although Franco denied that he was singling out British ships, this assurance was hardly any help since almost all shipping being done with the Republic was now being carried on British ships. On June 14, Chamberlain was asked in the Commons what protective measures were contemplated. There were numerous difficulties, he replied, for giving protection "to ships trading with ports in the war zone while they are in territorial waters, unless this country is prepared to take an active part in the hostilities." Although Chamberlain warned Franco that attacks could not continue without seriously injuring relations between their countries, it was clear, by what he wrote later, that any effective action could only be taken at the expense of risking war with Franco, ultimately perhaps with Germany and Italy; "of course, it may come to that if Franco were foolish enough." [2] Chamberlain insisted nothing could be done without endangering the country's true interests. He felt that whatever the incidents they did not justify forceful or retaliatory measures; the Government would have to be patient in the "face of accusations of weakness" and other methods, producing equally satisfactory results, would have to be found to free Great Britain from the danger of starting war. [3] In the following debate (June 21st), Labour as usual was more eager for action than the Conservatives. Colonel Wedgewood said,

If England is not respected by Italy, Germany, or France, if we lose the respect, which means a reasonable, decent fear, of the people who are war-makers, who believe in the use of force as against law to shape the fortunes of humanity, if we lose their respect, we lose that peace for which we and the democratic nations stand.

[1] Ibid., p. 212.
[2] Feiling, p. 352.
[3] BD., I, p. 619.

Butler retorted that the Government's policy was more realistic because it determined to keep the country out of war and save the peace and, stating the other half of the dichotomy, concluded,

It is impossible to save democracy by taking any risks of going to war, and the object of our dual policy of international conciliation and national strength, is to save our democracy from war and so retain it in peace.

Ciano's request for immediate effectuation of the Anglo-Italian accord had remained unanswered, until June 20th, when Lord Perth presented the Italians with three alternatives:

1. Execution of the plan of the Non-Intervention Committee.
2. Unilateral withdrawal of the Italian forces sent to Spain.
3. Armistice in Spain.[1]

Also, since Italy and France were directly connected with the situation in Spain and indirectly, through relations with Britain, with each other, Mussolini would reconsider, Chamberlain hoped, a resumption of the stillborn conversations with France. Doubtful of giving Britain satisfaction on any points, Ciano nevertheless agreed to discuss the matter with the Duce and reply in several days.

While Britain waited, more Nationalist attacks occurred. On June 28 Perth warned Ciano of the adverse effect these raids were having on British public opinion and on the eventual progress of Anglo-Italian relations; although Britain would still follow the policy of Non-Intervention, Chamberlain's position was being undermined by charges that he was unable to protect the interests of his own country. Ciano offered no encouragement and four days later he handed the British Ambassador a reply to the June 20th memorandum. Mussolini rejected all the British suggestions, and therefore the only remaining course was to "await the developments of events in Spain, either through the Committee of Non-Intervention or through the progress of the war, in order to apply the agreements of 16th April." [2] In bad humour because of a high fever, Ciano turned on poor Lord Perth, charging that it was the absence of British good faith which was holding up friendly relations; if unfortunate consequences resulted the onus was clearly on Great Britain, and until such time when the British put the agreement into effect, Italy would reserve full freedom of action. With almost a sense of pride he had written the day before "a crisis in our relations

---

[1] *Ciano's Diplomatic Papers*, p. 296.
[2] *Ibid.*, p. 221.

with London is almost inevitable." [1] Perth left completely depressed. This mood eventually affected the Prime Minister.

On July 5th the American Ambassador, Joseph Kennedy, found him generally pessimistic. Chamberlain felt although attacks on shipping had slowed down, there was no guarantee this would continue, and while there was no immediate danger for a new election or change of Government, if the people were to continue to read about attacks on British shipping they might become particularly troublesome. Chamberlain was mad he had to tolerate Mussolini's nonsense, bad temper and resentful attitude, but he repeatedly stressed "my job is to try to keep England out of the war if I possibly can; therefore, I am doing a lot of things that are difficult for me to do." If Mussolini changed his mind, Chamberlain hoped that he could persuade him to help settle the Spanish situation, but personally he was skeptical about the Duce's assurances. Kennedy was impressed by Chamberlain's apparent cheerfullness, but noted that "underneath there is great concern over the pressure that is being brought to bear on him." [2] It was in this frame of mind that Chamberlain prepared to answer Mussolini's discouraging *aide-mémoire*.

Presented to Ciano on July 11th, the British reply stated that a settlement in Spain (defined as effective withdrawal of volunteers) was a *sine qua non* for operation of the Anglo-Italian pact. The Government did not feel that delay would hurt the treaty. There were no alternatives and nothing could be done until Italian compliance.[3] The same day Britain published as a White Paper [4] the plan, accepted by the Non-Intervention Committee on July 5, 1938, for withdrawal of foreign combatants from Spain. The fifth such plan, a wholly revised version of the original submitted a year ago, this latest scheme, running to the impossible length of some eighty pages, closely printed, was an extremely detailed treatment of the entire evacuation process. Like previous efforts, though, approval did not imply operation, which demanded the consent of both Spanish Governments. As there was little chance Mussolini would use his influence with Franco, both sides consequently looked to events in Spain to solve their problem.

Public opinion demanded Chamberlain make no further concession on the question of volunteers. In the Commons July 26 defining a settlement of the Spanish situation Chamberlain said, "I would like to

[1] Ciano, *Journal Politique*, 217.
[2] *USD.*, 1938, I, p. 57.
[3] *Ciano's Diplomatic Papers*, pp. 225–226.
[4] *Cmd.* 5793.

see what happens, when the volunteers are withdrawn, if His Majesty's Government think that Spain has ceased to be a menace to the peace of Europe, I think we shall regard that as a settlement of the Spanish Question." In spite of the developing crisis in Eastern Europe, Labour showed itself still primarily concerned with events in Spain. On July 27, the National Council of Labour, commemorating the Second Anniversary of the outbreak of the war, made "an appeal to every British citizen who loves fair play" to denounce Non-Intervention. However, as in similar invocations, there was no mention of active intervention or help, other than contributing to certain established humanitarian activities. And later the Trade Union Congress, held at Blackpool on September 5th to the 9th, in spite of rumours to the contrary, did not wish to commit itself beyond a call for collective defense against aggression.

Privately, according to the French Foreign Minister, Bonnet,[1] the British had promised France they would "go to war if necessary to eject the Italians and Germans from any strategic position they might have acquired, and might refuse to give up." But Franco had "given categoric assurances to both Great Britain and France that if he should be victorious, neither the Italians nor the Germans would be left in the possession of any strategic position whatsoever in Spain," [2] and therefore Chamberlain hoped that this action would be unnecessary.

In autumn 1938, the Czechoslovak crisis gave the the British Government little time to consider Spanish affairs, but for France the war was made more immediate. Realizing the vulnerability of the Southern border to attack by German and Italian troops if Czechoslovakia touched off hostilities, the decision was taken to reinforce the Spanish frontier with several divisions. This move was directly represented by the yellow press as the first step towards intervention. The Prefect of the Pyrénées telegraphed the Ministry of the Interior that newsreel men were arriving in his *Département* to film the passage of French troops into Spain. A Cabinet meeting was called, the confusion of which was epitomized in Pétain's irrelevant remark, "Tout cela, c'est la faute de la semaine de quarante heures." [3] At Munich the evening of September 29th, finding Mussolini in a quiet and reserved frame of mind, and encouraged by his invitation to visit Rome, Chamberlain raised the question of Spain by suggesting that a truce and terms of settlement

[1] *USD., Papers*, 1938, I, p. 59.
[2] *Ibid.*, p. 59.
[3] *Evénements Survenus*, pp. 802–803.

could be achieved through the convocation of a Four-Power Conference. Mussolini said he would think it over, adding that Italy "would be prepared shortly to withdraw a substantial number of troops from Spain." [1] The next day Chamberlain reported this conversation to Hitler. He told him that Mussolini, claiming he had lost 50,000 troops in Spain was fed up with the war (to this Hitler laughed out loud), and was no longer afraid of Bolshevist domination there. Turning to Hitler, Chamberlain then asked whether the Führer had anything to say about the intention of Mussolini to consider withdrawal. Hitler began by saying that, although he had no territorial designs on Spain, his motive for intervention being only the support of Franco against Communism, he was not so sure that the threat of Bolshevism was over. "The Duce says so," interrupted Chamberlain.

Moreover, Hitler continued, he was unsure that it would be possible to induce the two parties in Spain to agree to a truce, but he agreed with Mussolini "that the end of the Spanish conflict would be welcome and he would be delighted to withdraw the few German volunteers who were there as soon as the others were willing to do the same." [2] When Hitler had finished, Chamberlain admitted that he was as much in the dark as the Führer about how to secure a truce, but he thought "that if the two sides received a call from the Four Great Powers, they might be induced to listen and that, once the truce had been called, the Powers might be able to help in getting a settlement." [3] Chamberlain had reason to feel that the Munich Conference had created a favourable atmosphere in respect to Italy; he had used, or so he thought, Mussolini as a pacifier of Hitler, but later wrote that the Duce "seemed to be cowed" by his German ally. Consequently, by strengthening Mussolini a more moderate balance could be given to the Axis. Sir Noel Charles, British *Chargé d'Affaires* in Rome, had previously urged placating Italy's "nuisance value" to restore an equilibrum to the Rome-Berlin Axis; he judged that Mussolini, being in no position to resist German diplomatic pressure, wished to free his hands by finalizing the Anglo-Italian agreement as soon as possible. There should be no hope of breaking the Axis or of expecting a lasting solution of their difficulties, but by making Italy a better bargain than she could temporarily get from Hitler, by putting the Anglo-Italian Pact into immediate force, Britain could restore the Axis to its proper propor-

[1] *BD.*, III, p. 314.
[2] *BD.*, II, pp. 636–637.
[3] *Ibid.*

tions and prevent any desperate move by Italy to throw in her lot completely with Germany.[1] For the moment though with British papers reporting new Italian troop movements there did not seem any way to act upon such advise.

On the 21st of September at the annual meeting of the League, Juan Negrin suddenly announced that the Republican Government had decided unilaterally, immediately and completely to withdraw all non-Spanish combatants. To prevent any attempt to transfer the supervision of these withdrawals to the Non-Intervention Committee, Negrin requested the League to establish a special International Commission. Britain had no objection and suggested that if that "other party" in Spain were to take similar steps they would be welcomed with the same spirit. Unknown at the time was Franco's decision to also effect the withdrawal, but only partly, of foreign troops, which, postponed several times because of the military situation (The Italians as well as Franco were apparently waiting for success of the current Catalonian offensive. The previous July the Republican forces had managed to stop the Insurgent advance by their counterattack across the Ebro. During September and October, despite persistent efforts only half the ground lost in July had been retaken.) was finally agreed upon on the first of October. The same day Ciano told Lord Perth that it would presently be possible to withdraw a whole division (10,000 men) which constituted half – according to British estimates one fourth – of their forces in Spain. When the British Ambassador asked why Italy was not able to withdraw all of their forces, Ciano replied, "this was hardly possible as the Italian Government did not wish to give the impression that they were completely abandoning Franco." [2] On October 2 a Foreign Office memorandum reported Mussolini's arrangements for troop withdrawal and said that since Mussolini will probably claim he is fulfilling British conditions for a settlement of the Spanish Question,

The problem before His Majesty's Government will then be whether the withdrawal was sufficiently "on a considerable scale" to justify to public opinion here recognition of the Italian Empire in Abyssinia in order to bring the Anglo-Italian Agreement into force.[3]

Subsequent conversations revealed the great importance that Italy placed on the British Treaty. Her arguments went from bribery to

---

[1] *USD.*, 1938, I, pp. 71–72.
[2] *BD.*, III, p. 312.
[3] *Ibid.*, p. 315.

blackmail and back to bribery: on October 3rd Ciano said that, after the agreement had come into force Italy would not only be willing to participate in a Four Power Conference, but might resume her negotiations with France; on October 4 he said unless the British Government was willing to put the treaty into force by the time the volunteers had reached Naples, Mussolini, instead of working for a general pacification of Europe, would conclude a military alliance with Germany; and on October 5 he said if the present Italian proposals were accepted, Mussolini would give formal assurances that no more troops were sent to Spain. Although Halifax was favourably disposed, he wanted it stressed "if there is no reduction of Italian air forces in Spain, and if bombing of British ships continues, we shall have considerable difficulty in carrying public opinion." [1]

Meanwhile, Francis Hemming, Secretary of the Non-Intervention Committee, had been sent to Burgos, charged with the task of explaining the British withdrawal plan while finding out Franco's intentions regarding its execution.[2] Britain informed Italy it would be extremely desirable if they were to use their influence with Franco to make him more cooperative toward the Non-Intervention Committee's proposals.[3] Chamberlain had promised Parliament that before final action bringing the Anglo-Italian pact into force there would be a general debate; therefore, pending the reopening of Parliament on November 1, he let matters temporarily rest. While waiting, using the Foreign Office to help prepare their case for Commons,[4] the Government tried to prevent any incidents, bombings, troop movements, etc. which could arouse public opinion. Mussolini, assured that the Anglo-Italian accord was successfully headed toward ratification and, feeling that he had lived up to his part of the agreement as much as he cared to, treated these efforts diffidently. Thus Lord Perth concluded it was useless for Britain "to expect Italian cooperation for any further measures connected with the cession of the Spanish war, apart from those agreed by the Non-Intervention Committee until the agreement has come into force." [5] On October 26, after a secret Cabinet meeting, the British Government informed Mussolini "in the strictest confidence" that they had decided to bring the agreement into force. After the Commons debate, the British Ambassador would henceforth be

---

[1] *Ibid.*, p. 326.
[2] *USD.*, 1938, I, pp. 243–244.
[3] *BD.*, III, p. 332.
[4] See report of October 15, 1938, by Perth; *Ibid.*, p. 339.
[5] *Ibid.*, p. 338.

accredited to the King of Italy *and* Emperor of Ethiopia.[1] Mussolini was pleased. In conversation with Ribbentrop two days later he joyfully said that he had no intention of ending material aid to Franco until the final victory.[2]

As no public announcement had been made on the recent negotiations, when Chamberlain proposed (on November 2nd) that the House welcome the Government's intention to bring the agreement into force, he created an atmosphere of surprise. With such short notice – no doubt intentional on Chamberlain's part – the Opposition had no chance to rally public opinion, but inadequate time in no way left them at a loss for words. Expressing Labour's general attitude Arthur Greenwood assailed Chamberlain's whole policy of appeasement,

> The Government are engaged in a crazy policy, whittling away the freedom of the people. They have already sacrificed Abyssinia; they have already sacrificed Austria; and within recent days they have sacrificed Czechoslovakia. Today they are in effect throwing Spain to the wolves in order to rehabilitate the shattered fortunes and the rather tarnished prestige of Signor Mussolini, regardless of the consequences to Spain, regardless of the possible consequences to ourselves, to democracy and the Empire in particular.[3]

On November 4th Mussolini personally telephoned Grandi and, in a voice of unconcealed joy and gratitude, told his Ambassador to convey to Chamberlain and Halifax his warm feeling of appreciation. In Rome, November 16, Count Ciano and Lord Perth formally signed the declaration bringing the Anglo-Italian treaty into effect. The date had been suggested three weeks previously by Ciano, who apparently felt a certain sense of propriety in having the agreement take effect on the same day of the month on which it was originally signed.

3. A GAME ENDING IN NO SCORE

Britain's hope that activation of the Anglo-Italian agreement would restore Mussolini the liberty of action he needed to equalize his position with Germany went unappreciated. Nevertheless Chamberlain believed he did the right thing; he did not always take Mussolini's word at face value, but he did tend to minimize the significance of Mussolini's deceptions. For example, in the foreign policy debate on December 19th,

---

[1] The French Ambassador, François-Poncet, had been accredited under the same credentials on October 4th, 1938.
[2] *Ciano's Diplomatic Papers*, p. 246.
[3] *Hansard*, 340, col. 217.

1938, Chamberlain made no attempt to deny that Italy since the conclusion of the agreement four weeks previously had sent reinforcements
of men and supplies to Spain, but he confidently announced that these
forces were too small to constitute an increase in Italian effectiveness
and did not therefore break any pledge which Italy had given. Refusing to abandon hope, in spite of all manifestations of hostility, Chamberlain pushed forward plans to visit Mussolini in Rome. "We are not
going to Rome," he said, "with any fixed agenda or with the expectation of bringing back any new specific agreement... we are going
with a desire to improve our relations... to strengthen confidence
between us." In his diary Chamberlain was more specific: "I don't
believe that Spain is a menace to European peace any longer, all the
same I should immensely like to stop the conflict there, and although
Mussolini wasn't very forthcoming on the subject at Munich, I got the
idea that it would be worthwhile to take it up with him again, after our
own agreement had come into force." [1]

The visit of January 11 to 13 was indecisive. Chamberlain was
impressed by his reception from the Italian people – mostly "in the
middle class section of the city, where the old man with the umbrella
is quite popular," [2] – but Mussolini's greeting was another matter.
Unconvinced from the start that the visit had any utility, he found the
conversations as dull as Chamberlain; in an aside to Ciano after dinner
the first evening, he remarked, "These men [Chamberlain and Halifax]
are not made of the same stuff as Francis Drake and the other mag-
nificent adventurers who created the Empire. These, after all, are
the tried sons of a long line of rich men and they will lose their Empire." [3]
(Chamberlain, however, wrote that he found Mussolini "straightforward
and considerate in his behaviour to us, and moreover, he has a sense of
humour which is quite attractive... He was emphatic in his assurance
that he intended to stand by his agreement with us, and that he wanted
peace, and was ready to use his influence to get it.") [4] The intention to
plan future conversations with Germany was not realized because
Italy was too solidly a part of the Axis; the intention to smooth affairs
in Spain was not realized because it was too late. Chamberlain had more
on his mind than a general attempt to pacify an already chilled dispute;
he knew the Republican cause lost and the Non-Intervention Committee
as good as finished. The only outstanding question was the withdrawal

[1] Feiling, p. 398.
[2] *Ciano Diaries*, p. 9.
[3] *Ibid.*, p. 20.
[4] Feiling, p. 393.

of volunteers, and although Chamberlain was not going to insist on evacuation this late in the war, he was definitely interested in Mussolini's assurance that he would fulfill this part of the Anglo-Italian Agreement. The trip to Rome therefore meant a further verification of Mussolini's intentions.

As if he anticipated this purpose at the beginning of the conversations, Mussolini "repeated emphatically that [Italy] intended to stand loyally by their obligations under the agreement, and rather went out of his way to stress that when the Spanish conflict was over, they would have nothing to ask from Spain." [1] The next morning in private conversation with Halifax, Ciano repeated the Duce's assurance saying that though Italy would "certainly try to get back anything they could through the channels of legitimate trade... they would seek no privileged position, and certainly, as they had frequently assured us, had no territorial designs." [2] Superfically Ciano reasoned if Italy had been after territorial concessions, it would have been obviously to her interest to have sought Spain's partition, which not being done should surely testify to an absence of ulterior motives. Commenting on Halifax's reaction, he wrote "He talks of politics with a certain impersonal interest... I repeated to him our point of view and he gave his. But he does not seem very convinced, and at heart I think he would be happy if Franco's victory were to settle the question." [3] Ciano failed to appreciate Britain's intentional resignation; Halifax did not have the good sense to conceal it. From the Italian point of view the talks were unproductive because they produced no new concessions; Mussolini and Ciano took a special delight in patronizing the British desire for peace which they regarded as a mask for interests no longer defensible. Chamberlain though returned from Rome, achieving all that he had expected. "I am satisfied," he wrote, "that the journey had definitely strengthened the chances of peace." [4]

Meanwhile news from Spain, increasingly black for the Republic, provoked "Arms for Spain" demonstrations in France and Britain; word circulated that France would not tolerate Franco's capture of Barcelona. Ciano telephoned Lord Perth and asked him to urge the French to be moderate and to realize the sense of responsibility the situation demanded; he threatened if there were intervention the Italians would attack Valencia. "Thirty battalions, fully equipped, are

[1] *BD.*, III, p. 518.
[2] *Ibid.*, p. 522.
[3] *Ciano Diaries*, p. 10.
[4] Feiling, p. 393.

ready to be embarked at the first sign. We shall do this even if it should provoke a European war." [1] But Ciano's concern was unnecessary. Even if she had wanted to, France would not have acted without Great Britain. Blum had always made this clear and there was no change under Chautemps or Daladier. (On August 1st 1938, Leon Blum had publicly said that on the question of Spain, London gave the initiative and it was their policy that determined in the last resort the position of the French Government.[2] Later, the French Foreign Minister, Georges Bonnet remarked that the basis of French Foreign Policy, to maintain close cooperation with Britain, made it difficult for his country to have a clear Spanish policy.)[3] When Britain informed the French about their Rome conversations, Bonnet did not give the impression that France had been considering any radical policy departures; for the moment she was willing to accept present circumstances. The French Foreign Minister emphasized that at no point should any doubt "arise in the Italian mind of the importance... attached to the fulfillment of [their] undertakings." [4] But even as he spoke the end of the war was near.

Barcelona capitulated January 26, 1939; and refugees – variously estimated from 35,000 to 200,000 – streamed Northward to France. "The tide," wrote a British correspondent, "is made up of women and babies and children and old people and cripples and wounded civilians and a large number of wounded soldiers. All ages, all types – the tradesman, the peasant, the visibly once well-to-do, and of those who have been refugees already in some other part of the country, who have lost everything in Asturias, Bilbao, Malaga, Madrid, Barcelona." [5] Mussolini could hardly contain his pleasure; appearing on the balcony at the Palazzo Venezia he told the crowd: "The troops of Franco and our intrepid legionnaires have beaten not only the Negrin Government, but many others among our enemies are biting the dust." [6] Ciano, ever the sycophant, wrote: "Victory in Spain bears only one name, that is the name of Mussolini, who conducted the campaign bravely, firmly, even at a time when many people who now applaud him were against him." [7] The fall of Catalonia, followed on February 5th by the flight of the Republican Government to France, raised questions of recognition. Although the Loyalist cause was clearly lost, Chamberlain

[1] *Ciano's Diplomatic Papers*, p. 13.
[2] Blum, p. 192.
[3] *USD.*, 1938, I, p. 59.
[4] *BD.*, III, p. 530.
[5] *Guardian*, February. 3, 1939.
[6] *Ibid.*
[7] *Ciano Diaries*, p. 16.

thought that by delaying recognition he could help the Republicans get promises of clemency from Franco. (The Republic had stated that they were prepared to surrender on the condition that Franco would agree to the immediate withdrawal of foreign troops, the establishment of a representative government, and an amnesty for Republican supporters.) Britain's primary interest, however, was still the rapid liquidation of foreign interests.

The early part of February, to head off a possible Italian attempt to help Franco capture Minorca, the British helped to negotiate a surrender. The best harbour in the Balearics was Port Mahon in Minorca, which, being the furthest island East, was not only the closest to Italy, but was in the direct path of French shipping to North Africa. The port had been fortified by a British firm before the war and might have been difficult for Franco to assault without foreign help. On February 9th, therefore, while Nationalist troops occupied the island, the British cruiser *Devonshire* took on board 450 Loyalist refugees.[1] A note of strength was added concurrently by Chamberlain's declaration "that the whole force of Britain would co-operate if there were any threat to the vital interests of France." [2] Chamberlain did not want negotiations for surrender to drag on too long. He was optimistic that Britain would be able "to establish excellent relations with Franco." On February 13th the British Cabinet authorized Chamberlain to recognize *de jure* Nationalist Spain at a time he would judge convenient. (Britain wanted joint recognition with the French. But France was anxious to obtain concessions from Franco before recognition and it was only under pressure of Britain that this position was ultimately dropped.) [3] On February 22nd a telegram arrived from Nationalist Spain saying that although Franco demanded unconditional surrender, his patriotism, chilvalry and generosity and "likewise the spirit of justice which inspires all the National Government's actions, constitute a firm guarantee for all Spaniards who are not criminals." [4] The British Government did not feel it to their advantage to prolong recognition any longer; although Franco's telegram had made no promises Britain, in a weak position to insist too strongly on conditions, could only hope that Franco were sincere. Thus on February 27th Chamberlain announced the British Government's decision to unconditionally recognize the Nationalist Government. In Burgos, General Franco

[1] *Survey*, 1938, I, pp. 300–301; *GD.*, pp. 835–836.
[2] Feiling, p. 393.
[3] *Survey*, 1938, I, pp. 346–348.
[4] *Ibid.*, p. 302

exhaled, "The hour of truth has come. Today England recognizes us. Tomorrow it will be the world." Labour, as usual, introduced a motion of censure.

March saw the complete collapse of the Republic; Madrid surrendered the 28th, Valencia, Cartagena and Albacete the next day. In 48 hours the third of Spain still in Republican hands gave up. Now the question could no longer be avoided. Would the foreign armies leave Spain voluntarily? (It should be remembered that the Germans, unlike the Italians, never made any formal commitment that their troops would be withdrawn after the end of the war. This fact, having been the subject of several parliamentary questions, was finally admitted by Under-Secretary of State Butler on May 11, 1938.) By the war's official end on April 1st, neither Germany nor Italy seemed to be in a particular hurry to withdraw their forces. On April the 7th the situation was made more acute by the Italian invasion of Albania,[1] which seemed to discredit all Mussolini's commitments under the Anglo-Italian Pact. On April the 9th following several attempted inquiries, the Foreign Office was informed that Mussolini would withdraw his "volunteers" as soon as the victory parade was held in Madrid, and "as soon as the troops were withdrawn Italian aeroplanes and pilots would leave also." [2] But as the date for this intended pageant suspiciously lacked precision, Sir Arthur Sinclair remarked in the Commons on 13 april 1939.

> We are told that first of all they must join in a victory march through Madrid. Then we ask when the victory march is to take place... We are told that unfortunately General Franco has influenza and that the victory march has to be postponed. Then we are told that it is to be post-poned until the end of this month or the beginning of May, and afterwards, we are told that the troops must have 10 days to rest after their fatiguing march to Madrid, and that the evacuation will begin about the 10th of May... When is this victory march to take place and when is the evacuation of Italian troops from Spain to begin? We ought surely to be told that.

Matters were complicated by rumors that Mussolini was actually sending fresh reinforcements; and Göring, in the grand manner of Wilhelm II, decided to accompany German fleet maneuvers off Spanish waters. The victory parade was postponed again, first until May 15th, then to the 19th, after which, undoubtedly to the surprise of many, the evacuations began, while bunting still hung in Madrid streets. The Italian legionnaires arrived home June 5th, the Germans a day later.

---

[1] Also on the same day Franco announced his adherence to the Anti-Comintern Pact.
[2] Hansard, 346, col. 14.

They were gone but international unrest remained. When the new British Ambassador, Percy Loraine, was received in Rome, Mussolini told him "that British politics were leading the whole of Europe into war." [1] The war that Britain had tried so desperately to avoid was near and the Britons who had concluded that the Spanish conflict was but a rehearsal found it poor consolation to be right.

[1] *Ciano Diaries*, p. 88.

CONCLUSION

British policy required the containment of the war and the preservation of Spanish integrity; both were realized. Since success implies
the realization of aims British policy was successful. If Britain had
been deliberately able to control the outcome of events, her policy
would have been masterful, but this was not the case. Except where her
immediate interests were concerned, her reaction to challenge was
conscious abdication. While by no means invalid, such a policy does
come at a price, which, as circumstances disclosed, was high, but as
history revealed was not, although almost, too high. It is easier for
the historian to explain, just as it is for the reader to judge, a policy
of strength than one of weakness; sins of omission, if indeed nations
do sin, are more difficult to assess than those of commission. Since
all foreign policy is selfish, it does little good to condemn Britain for
a lack of altruism towards Spain. Britain was disposed towards a
weak policy for reasons both psychological and practical.

The British attitude towards Spain had been set by the Duke of
Wellington one hundred and thirty years before. "There is no country
in Europe," he had said, "in the affairs of which foreigners can interfere with so little advantage as in those of Spain." In terms of British
internal affairs these words took on a new meaning during the Thirties,
a decade of diminishing hope, when to seek refuge, an identity from
an insecure existence, people found comfort in mass movements.

Although for the most part extremism had minor attraction for the
average Briton, Spanish affairs so ideologically loaded emphasized
that above all any considered policy should help Britain preserve her
traditional institutions and social constancy. One might say that the
policy of Non-Intervention although in practice encouraging confusion,
contradiction and insincerity, was still a policy which divided the
British people least. The cause of Spain from this standpoint was just

about the worst possible upon which to provoke a war. It was equally inadvisable from the aspect of military preparedness.

While it thus would have been desirable to have the practice of Non-Intervention commensurate with its theory, once the agreement seemed, even imperfectly, to serve the main purpose of containing the war, it was further compromised but not abolished and British action when not concentrated on removing Fascist influence around Franco, tried to bridge a gap between interventionist powers thereby controlling, if not preventing, their intervention. The policy operated with one eye always on the power struggle produced by the war, and the tendency not to have meetings when Franco was winning, suggest an ulterior use of the Committee.[1] After all, Non-Intervention was primarily the responsibility of the British Conservative party, run on the average by the upper middle class, which within certain limits was indifferent to the form of Spanish government as long as it did not threaten British interests. But, in so far as indigenous Communism was more dangerous in the long run than indigenous Fascism, they were likely to prefer Franco to a more suspicious alternative. In this sense, and also by virtue of the fact that the Non-Intervention policy, although conceived of as neutrality, worked in favour of one side, the Government's attitude was pro-Nationalist. It was not without justification that Labour charged the Government with waiting for an Insurgent victory to solve her problems; it is fairly clear from the statements of British rulers that the Fascist demand for a Franco victory was accepted with, if nothing else, at least resignation. And it is indeed true that, given the fact of the war, Franco's chances of restoring internal stability appeared better than those of his opponents.

Since Britain regarded the war as an issue in itself, it is more difficult to relate it to her overall policy, although the practice has been to oversimplify it as just another part of appeasement. Given her internal situation and commitments elsewhere, there was nothing dishonest in Britain's dismissal of Spain, but isolation of this sort, minimizing certain of the war's side effects, badly warped judgments on the policy's far-reaching consequences. Individuals were often at cross-purposes; institutions became dumping grounds for responsibility and the results were highly ambivalent and unpredictable. The Non-Intervention Committee not only helped to contain the war but it also brought Mussolini and Hitler closer together. The war itself sapped Mussolini's strength while it built up Hitler's. On the one hand Britain

[1] See Chronology.

created an opportunity for Franco to escape from the dictator's clutches, and on the other she failed to exploit Italian weakness when occasions arose. It was ironical that Great Britain, the most vocal defender of collective security, should have had the major role in destroying the League. However, the real key to British weakness seems to be in her dealings with Italy.

Britain negotiated with Mussolini to achieve the same objectives mentioned earlier: to remove the danger of war and Italy's permanent influence in Spain. British techniques though were too candid; Chamberlain's extremely open manner was both harmful and unnecessary. On one occasion, for example, he solicited the Duce's approval of a speech he would make in the Commons,[1] and occasionally he was more frank with Mussolini than with his own Parliament. The Foreign Office in October 1938 estimated the number of Italian troops in Spain at 40,000, Chamberlain preferred instead Mussolini's figure of 20,000.[2] The Government's lack of subtlety was severely criticized by Lloyd George in a famous answer to the continual argument "do you want war?" If that is taken, he said,

as an indication of our attitude, as far as the majority of the House is concerned, a foreign power can safely defy us in any policy which we may take up. Whether we will go to war or not is a matter which we must keep to ourselves and judge for ourselves; but beforehand, to proclaim to the world that whatever other nations, do, at any rate as far as the majority of the House is concerned, they would not countenance war, is a great diplomatic weakness.[2]

However, in spite of the truth of Lloyd George's words, it is hard to call British policy toward Italy on the question of the Civil War a failure. On the contrary, her aims were achieved. It is true that Mussolini, knowing Britain was primarily interested in complete withdrawal only after the war, took a more contemptuous attitude of British proposals than he might otherwise have, but the fact remains that the emphasis on withdrawal was vindicated as was hoped. In tangible concessions, both sides surrendered very little. It is true Britain recognized the Italian Empire without receiving concessions on Spain in return, but this formality after all was small. British failure to keep Mussolini neutral cannot be blamed entirely on Britain's spirit of abdication, for in reality what had she to offer Mussolini? Hitler had army maneuvers, flag wavings and mass hysteria; he could promise

---

[1] *Ciano Diaries*, p. 17.
[2] *BD.*, p. 315, 319.
[3] *Hansard*, 325, col. 1591.

Mussolini support for his ambitions in a way impossible to Britain. Britain had nothing to give because she had what Mussolini wanted. Hitler had everything to give because he could give what he did not have. It is doubtful that Mussolini would have been satisfied with much less than the ruin of British power in the Mediterranean.

A favourite argument runs that neither Mussolini nor Hitler were prepared to go to war over Spain and therefore had Britain threatened force both would have backed down. During the first two months of the Civil War there is much to be said for the truth of this claim, although there were reasons why Britain failed to act; however, once the opportunity was missed, it is doubtful whether it could have been achieved without great risks. While Hitler, his interest focused on the East, not the Southwest, could conceivably have backed down, Mussolini's case is a bit different. Is it logical to assume that a man who took his country into war over the combined opposition of Ciano, the Italian General Staff, the Royal Family plus numerous officials in the Fascist Government, [1] would not have made a similar blunder if forced into a corner by Great Britain earlier? Too often Mussolini is treated as a buffoon and a bluffer. Referring to both dictators, Ward Price observed, "Gamblers they may be, but not bluffers – for even if their hand were weak, they would rather overturn the table than allow it to be called." [2] Although it was not Hitler's intention to make Spain a *casus belli*, it was to his interest to keep Mussolini involved in Spain as long as possible to cover his ambitions in Eastern Europe; an Italian war with England would have served the purpose as well. It obviously would have been more to the interest of Mussolini to have accepted British overtures for a general Mediterranean settlement than to have rejected them for a junior partnership with Hitler, but dictators do not necessarily know what is best.

British statesmen, who had trouble understanding the dictators of the 20th Century, found an exception in Franco, surrounded by the traditional allies of Spanish reaction closer to Ferdinand VII than Benito Mussolini. Given Chamberlain's background, it is not too difficult to see why he had more success with the one than with the other. Diplomacy is an art of calculated guessing and Britain, acting on her assumptions, was able to create a feeling of mutual interest which helped to achieve in Franco's case what in Mussolini's failed.

The notable success of British policy came at Nyon. The problems

---

[1] Wells, pp. 117–118.
[2] Price, p. 250.

arose out of the Civil War, but its solution was not related to it. Nyon was intended as a warning to Mussolini that although his intervention in Spain would be tolerated, his challenge to British interest was another matter and would be dealt with separately. It was unfortunate that Britain let the matter rest there, for Nyon could have been used, not as has been suggested as a first step for the enforcement of Non-Intervention, but more importantly as a beginning of a stronger alliance with France. (Because of British action in the Non-Intervention Committee Russia had already been pushed into isolation.) Chamberlain though, having observed the French attitude toward the Rhineland crisis and observing the vacillation of the Popular Front, dismissed the French as weak. British feeling, therefore, remained essentially insular. In January 1938, Chamberlain wrote: "our people see that in the absence of a powerful ally, and until our armaments are completed, we must adjust our foreign policy to our circumstances, and even bear with patience and good humour actions which we should like to treat in a very different fashion." [1] Clearly demonstrating this attitude in Non-Intervention, Britain provoked boldness in her adversaries; her policy would have been in any case conciliatory, but to back down even before risks became apparent was a concession and loss of flexibility no nation should afford.

[1] Feiling, p. 324.

CHRONOLOGY

More than an ordinary list of dates, this chronology emphasizes the inter-connection of work done in the Non-Intervention Committee with the changing relationship of power in Spain. As Franco became more successful or when the military situation was indetermined, the Non-Intervention Committee found reason to meet infrequently. This practice of wait and see could take the form of active and intentional sabotage practiced by Italy or a not so zealous acquiescence indulged in by Great Britain; both procedures though could produce equal effects. Non-Intervention's notorious protractions, seemingly taken for granted by all participants, make it difficult to believe, in spite of protestations to the contrary, that anyone concerned expected or wished the Committee to be really different from the way it was: "a theoretical guardian of a fictitious neutrality." [1]

Events of Non-Intervention	*Events in Spain and Britain*

1936

The Birth of Non-Intervention	*The Campaign North from Seville*
Aug. 1 — France proposes Non-Intervention; notes sent to London and Rome.	Aug. — Of 47 Spanish provinces, Nationalists control 19, Republic 25, undecided 3.
Aug. 4 — Britain replies favourably.	Aug. 14 — Franco captures Badajoz.
Aug. 19 — Britain unilaterally prohibits the export of war materials to Spain.	Aug. 26 — Labour leaders discuss Spain with Eden and Halifax at Foreign Office.
Aug. 24 — All primarily interested powers have accepted Non-Intervention.	
Aug. 26 — France proposes the establishment of the Non-Intervention Committee (NIC) in London.	
Aug. 28 — All primarily interested powers have declared arms embargos.	

---

[1] Baumont, p. 714.

Procedural Preliminaries

Sept. 9 — First meeting of Non-Intervention Committee.

Sept. 14 — Appointment of Chairman's Sub-Committee (CSC).

Sept. 28 — Portugal sends a representative to the NIC.

Sept. 3 — Talavera falls to the Nationalists.

Sept. 11 — In London a 731 lb tuna is cooked whole at the Trocadero.

Sept. 13 — Nationalists enter San Sebastian.

Sept. 28 — Siege of Alcazar at Toledo is raised.

Charges of Violations

Oct. 9 — NIC begins discussion of charges that Germany, Italy and Portugal are violating the agreement.

Oct. 12 — Russian demand for further meeting denied by Lord Plymouth for lack of evidence.

Oct. 23 — Russia tells NIC that she does not consider herself bound by Non-Intervention to any greater extent than any other Governments.

Oct. 28 — NIC deadlocked on question of charges, decides it is impossible to prove allegations.

Oct. 5–9 — Labour Party Conference at Edinburgh.

Franco continues his advance on Madrid while Mola concentrates on the reduction of the Basque Provinces. Reports predict Republican collapse within a month.

Oct. 29 — Labour formally abandons their support of Non-Intervention.

Schemes of Control

Nov. 12 — NIC starts discussion on question of control.

Nov. 13 — Control by observation given provisional acceptance, but Germany and Italy temporize by demanding a scheme of air control.

Nov. 6 — Nationalist forces arrive on outskirts of Madrid, attack on capital begins.

Nov. 18 — Germany and Italy recognize Franco.

Nov. 23 — Insurgent attack on Madrid stopped in University City.

Control and Question of Volunteers

Dec. 2 — NIC decides to extend Non-Intervention to include volunteers.

Dec. 4 & 7 — Britain in CSC wants volunteer problem to have special examination; Germany and Italy are opposed.

Dec. 22 — On German suggestion CSC appoints technical sub-committees to handle volunteers and financial aspects, thus creating further opportunities for delay.

Dec. 24 — British-French démarche in Berlin, Lisbon, Rome, Moscow for solving the question of volunteers receives unfavourable replies.

1937

The NIC continues to work on control plans, which are submitted to the Governments in Spain. On the 19th Franco declares the plan unacceptable; since Germany and Italy are in favour of control before prohibition, the Committee devotes its time to finding an acceptable revision.

Jan. 28 — CSC reaches provisional agreement on revised control plan.

Jan. 2 — Gentleman's Agreement.

Campaign in Castille

Feb. 20 — Prohibition of dispatch and enlistment of volunteers comes into effect, but depends on good faith for enforcement.

March 8 — NIC gives final approval to land and sea supervision.

March 23 — In CSC Grandi refuses to discuss volunteer question, makes it clear that there will be no withdrawal until the end of the war.

March 24 — Russia attacks Italy in NIC, demands special commission go to Spain to verify its accusations; matter though is only referred back to CSC.

Feb. 6 — Nationalists start offensive on Jarama front.

March — Nationalists control 23 provinces, the Republicans 17, undecided 7.

March 13 — Nationalists begin attack on Guadalajara front, which ends in Italian rout a week later.

Campaign in the North

April 15 — After 3 week recess during which Britain tries to prevent breakdown of Committee by attempting direct persuasion, NIC appoints technical sub-committee to draft withdrawal plan.

April 30 — Control Scheme goes into full operation.

May — During the first three weeks of May the CSC discusses the Nationalist interference with shipping.

May 26 — Technical sub-committee submits detailed report on withdrawal, giving ways and means of supervision.

April 2 — Franco attacks the Basques.

April 26 — Guernica bombed.

May 28 — Baldwin resigns; Chamberlain becomes Prime Minister.

May 29 — *Deutschland* incident.

May 31 — Almeria shelled.

May 31 — Germany and Italy announce withdrawal from control scheme and Non-Intervention. Talks on withdrawal of volunteers virtually suspended.

June 16 — After reaching agreement against future attacks, Italy and Germany rejoin the Non-Intervention Committee and naval control.

June 20 — In CSC, Lord Plymouth presents new British proposals for withdrawal.

June 23 — Germany and Italy definitively leave the naval patrol.

June 14 — Britain, in an effort to resolve the problems created by Italo-German naval control withdrawal, presents the NIC with a compromise which couples withdrawal of volunteers with granting of belligerent rights.

July 20 — Discussion of British plan produces a deadlock; the question is debated in subsequent meetings.

Aug. 6 — British proposal in CSC to consider restoration of full naval control.

Aug. 27 — After no meeting for three weeks the prepared report holds that a continuation of naval control is in its present form not worth the expense.

Work of NIC superceeded by piracy in Mediterranean.

Sept. 17 — Non-Intervention naval control is terminated.

June 18 — The *Leipzig* allegedly attacked.

June 19 — Nationalists capture Bilbao.

June 22 — Eden says in Commons that Britain might reconsider their attitude if Non-Intervention affairs continue without success.

July 6 — Republican attacks West of Madrid result in capture of Brunete.

July 24 — Brunete retaken by Nationalists.

Aug. 26 — Surrender of Santander to Nationalists

Sept. 1 — British destroyer *Havock* attacked.

Sept. 7 — Start of Nyon Conference.

Sept. — Nationalists control 26 provinces, Republicans 15, undecided 6.

Question of Volunteers Again

Oct. 16 — CSC resumes work on withdrawal of volunteers. France demands success or will resume liberty of action.

Nov. 4 — After 2 weeks work NIC accepts in principle the British plan of July 14, but even though in turn accepted by Franco and the Loyalists, the year closes with still no substantial progress being made.

Oct. 15 — At Llandudno Eden declares British at end of their patience.

Oct. 21 — Gijon, Quiedo and Avila fall to Nationalists.

Nov. 16 — Britain sends Hodgson as her representative to Burgos.

Dec. 7 — Labour party openly desire Republican victory, Attlee visiting Spain.

1938

January — Discussion of British plan in CSC produces a deadlock which the NIC tries to resolve.

Jan. 11 — Authorization to Lord Plymouth to start private negotiations on withdrawal question.

March 31 — Discussion of British plan resumed. In CSC, Lord Plymouth remarks that recent developments put their work "in a somewhat different light."

CSC meets infrequently, during May there is a continuation of outside attempts to get acceptance of the British plan.

May 26 — Discussions again held in CSC, but sideline diplomacy continues.

June 30 — CSC record full agreement of British plan, revised.

July 5 — NIC, not having met since Nov. 4, 1937, meets for last time to approve British plan, which would take six months to make effective, not counting delays.

July 23 — British plan accepted by Republicans, but Franco procrastinates.

Oct. 11 — Francis Hemming sent to Burgos to discuss withdrawal plan with Franco. Lord Plymouth has declared at the end of August that there will be no purpose in summoning the NIC or CSC to discuss this question. From this time onward NIC is dead.

Campaign in Aragon

Jan. 8 — Republican offensive sweeps Teruel.

Feb. 20 — Eden resigns, replaced by Lord Halifax five days later.

Feb. 21 — Nationalists re-capture Teruel.

March 22 — Nationalists open offensive on Huesca front.

April 15 — Nationalists cut Republic in two at Vinaroz, advance subsequently towards Valencia.

April 16 — Anglo-Italian Agreement signed.

July — Provinces controlled by Nationalists 30; by Republicans 10; undecided 7.

July 24 — Republicans counter attack across Ebro.

Oct. 15 — Withdrawal of 10,000 Italian troops.

Nov. 16 — Anglo-Italian Agreement comes into force.

Dec. 23 — Nationalist attacks start to threaten Barcelona.

1939

March 1 — Russia withdraws from NIC.

March 22 — Germany and Italy refuse to pay anymore to NIC.

April 20 — Final meeting of NIC to dissolve itself.

Jan. 26 — Nationalists enter Barcelona.

Feb. 27 — Britain recognizes Franco.

April 1 — End of war.

BIBLIOGRAPHY

I. SOURCES

Documents

British Foreign Policy, Documents on, Ed. E. L. Woodward and Rohan Butler, Third Series, 1938–1939. (London 1950–1952.)
British White Papers, Command Papers, 1936–1939.
Chambre des Députés, Journal Officiel, 1936–1939.
Ciano's Diplomatic Papers, Ed. Malcom Muggeridge, (London 1948).
Evénements Survenus en France 1933–1945, Les, Rapport fait au nom de la Commission de l'Assemblée Nationale, (Paris 1951).
German Foreign Policy, Documents on, 1918–1945, Series D, Volume III, Germany and the Spanish Civil War 1936–1939, (Washington 1950).
Hansard, House of Commons Debates 1936–1939;
— House of Lords Debates 1936–1939.
International Affairs 1936–1939, Documents on, Royal Institute of International Affairs, (London 1937–1943).
International Conciliation Documents, (New York 1936–1939).
Labour Party Annual Conference Report 1936–1938, (London 1937–1939).
League of Nations, Official Journal, Monthly Summary, 1936–1939.
Padelford, Norman J., *International Law and Diplomacy in the Spanish Civil Strife*, (New York 1939).
Soviet Documents on Foreign Policy, Vol. III, Ed. Jane Degras, (London 1953).
United States, Foreign Relations of the, Diplomatic Papers, 1936, Vol. II; 1937, Vol. I; 1938, Vol. I; 1939, Vol. II, (Washington 1954–1956).

Memoirs, Speeches, Annuals, etc.

Alvarez Del Vayo, Julio, *Freedom's Battle*, (New York 1940);
— *The Last Optimist*, (New York 1950).
Amery, Leopold, *My Political Life*, Vol. III, (London 1955).
Attlee, Clement, *As it Happened*, (London 1954).
Bessie, Alvah, Ed. *The Heart of Spain*, Veterans of the Abraham Lincoln Brigade (New York 1952).
Blondel, Jules François, *Au Fil de la Carrière*, (Paris 1960).
Blum, Léon, *L'Histoire Jugera*, (Montreal 1943).
Bonnet, Georges, *De Washington au Quai D'Orsay*, (Geneva 1946);
— *Fin d'une Europe*, (Geneva 1948).

Boncour, Joseph Paul, *Entre Deux Guerres*, (Paris 1946).
Borkenau, Franz, *The Spanish Cockpit*, (London 1937).
Bowers, Claude G., *My Mission to Spain*, (New York 1954).
British Yearbook of International Law, 1937–1938 (Oxford).
Cerruti, Elisabeth, *Je les ai bien connus*, (Paris 1950).
Chamberlain, Neville, *The Struggle for Peace*, (London 1939).
Chatfield, Lord, *It Might Happen Again*, (London 1947).
Churchill, Winston, *The Gathering Storm*, (London 1948).
Ciano, Count, *Diaries*, 1939–1943 (New York 1946);
— *Journal Politique*, (Paris 1949).
Cooper, Duff, *Old Men Forget* (London 1953).
Cot, Pierre, *The Triumph of Treason*, (New York 1944).
Daladier, Edouard, *In Defense of France* (New York 1939).
Dalton, Hugh, *The Fateful Years*, (London 1957).
Dell, Robert, *The Geneva Racket*, (Bristol 1941).
Eden, Anthony, *Foreign Affairs*, (London 1939).
Epstein, Mortimer, Ed. *The Annual Register*, Vols. 178–181, (London 1937–1940).
Fisher, Louis, *Men and Politics*, (New York 1946).
Flandin, Pierre-Etienne, *Politique Française 1919–1940*, (Paris 1947).
François-Poncet, André, *Souvenirs d'une Ambassade à Berlin*, (Paris 1946);
— *Au Palais Farnèse*, (Paris 1961).
Gamelin, Général, *Servir: Le Prologue du Drame 1930–1939*, (Paris 1946).
Goebbels, Joseph, *Diaries*, (London 1948).
Halifax, Lord, *Speeches on Foreign Policy*, (London 1940);
— *Fullness of Days*, (London 1957).
Hassell, Ulrich von, *Diaries 1938–1944*, (London 1948).
Henderson, Sir Neville, *Failure of a Mission*, (London 1940).
Hoare, Sir Samuel, See Lord Templewood.
Hodgson, Sir Robert, *Spain Resurgent*, (London 1953).
Hull, Condell, *Memoirs*, Vol. I, (New York 1948).
Hyde, Douglas, *I Believed*, (London 1951).
Ismay, Lord, *Memoirs*, (London 1960).
Jellinek, Frank, *The Civil War in Spain*, (London 1938).
Koestler, Arthur, *Spanish Testament*, (London 1937).
Krivitsky, Walter G., *In Stalin's Secret Service*, (New York 1939).
Low, David, *Years of Wrath, A Cartoon History*, (London 1949).
Martin, Kingsley, *Harold Laski*, (London 1953).
Matthews, Herbert, *Two Wars and More to Come*, (New York 1939).
Minney, Rubreigh, *The Private Papers of Hore-Belisha*, (London 1960).
Morrison, Herbert, *Autobiography*, (London 1960).
Nenni, Pietro, *La Guerre d'Espagne* (Paris 1959).
Orwell, George, *Homage to Catalonia*, (London 1938).
Paul, Elliott H., *The Life and Death of a Spanish Town*, (London 1937).
Papen, Franz von, *Memoirs*, (London 1952).
Peterson, Maurice, *Both Sides of the Curtain*, (London 1950).
Price, G. Ward, *I Know These Dictators*, (London 1937).
Reynaud, Paul, *La France a sauvé l'Europe*, (Paris 1947).
Ribbentrop, Joachim von, *Memoirs*, (London 1954).
Rolfe, Edwin, *The Lincoln Battalion*, (New York 1939).
Rust, William, *Britons in Spain*, (London 1937).
Schmidt, Paul, *Hitler's Interpreter*, (London 1951).
Selby, Walford, *Diplomatic Twilight*, (London).

Simon, Viscount, *Retrospect, Memoirs*, (London 1952).
Suñer, Ramon Serrano, *Entre les Pyrénées et Gibraltar*, (Geneva 1949).
Temperly, Maj.-General, *The Whispering Gallery of Europe*, (London 1938).
Templewood, Lord, *Ambassador on Special Mission*, (London 1946);
— *Nine Troubled Years*, (London 1954).
Toynbee, Arnold, Ed., *Survey of International Affairs*, 1937, Vol. II, 1938, Vol. I;
 Royal Institute of International Affairs, (London 1938 and 1948).
Vansittart, Robert, *The Mist Procession*, (London 1958).
Wells, Sumner, *The Time for Decision*, (London 1945).
Wintringham, Tom, *English Captain*, (London 1939).

Newspapers and Periodicals

Contemporary Review
Current History
Daily Express
Daily Herald
Economist
L'Europe Nouvelle
Foreign Affairs
Fortnightly
Fortune
International Affairs
Journal de Genève
Lloyds Bank Review

London Times, Weekly Times
Manchester Guardian
Nation
New Statesman and Nation
New York Times
Observer
Political Quarterly
Quarterly Review
Spectator
Le Temps
World Review
Yale Review

2. WORKS

Biographies, Historical and Special Studies

Atholl, Duchess of, *Searchlight on Spain*, (London 1938).
Blythe, Henry, *Spain over Britain*, (London 1937).
Borkenau, Franz, *World Communism*, (New York 1939).
Baumont, Maurice, *La Faillite de la Paix*, Vol. II, (Paris 1960).
Bolloten, Burnett, *The Grand Camouflage*, (London 1961).
Brome, Vincent, *Aneurin Bevan*, (London 1953).
Broué, Pierre and Emile Temimé, *La Révolution et la Guerre d'Espagne*, (Paris 1961).
Bullock, Alan, *The Life and Times of Ernest Bevin*, Vol. 1, (London 1960).
Campbell-Johnson, Alan, *Viscount Halifax*, (London 1941);
— *Eden, the Making of a Statesman*, (New York 1955).
Carr, Edward H., *Britain*, (London 1939);
— *The Twenty Years Crisis*, (London 1939);
— *International Relations Between the Wars*, (London 1959).
Cattell, David T., *Communism and the Spanish Civil War*, (Berkley 1955);
— *Soviet Diplomacy and the Spanish Civil War*, (Berkley 1957).
Chavet, Jean F., *L'Influence Britannique dans la S.D.N.*, (Paris 1938).
Churchill, Randolph, *The Rise and Fall of Sir Anthony Eden*, (London 1959).
Cole, G. D. H., *The Peoples Front*, (London 1940).
Connell, John (John Henry Robertson), *The Office* (London 1958).
Cooke, Colin, *The Life of Richard Stafford Cripps*, (London 1957).
Craig, Gordon and Felix Gilbert, Eds., *The Diplomats*, (Princeton 1953).
Davies, John L., *Behind the Spanish Barricades*, (New York 1937).

East, Gordon, *Mediterranean Problems*, (London 1940).
Esch, Patricia van der, *Prelude to War*, (The Hague 1951).
Feiling, Keith, *The Life of Neville Chamberlain*, (London 1946).
Francis, E. V., *Britain's Economic Strategy*, (London 1939).
Fremantle, Anne, *This Little Band of Prophets*. (New York 1960).
Garrett, G. T., *Mussolini's Roman Empire*, (London 1938);
— *Gibraltar and the Mediterranean*, (London 1939).
Graves, Robert and Alan Hodge, *The Long Weekend*, (London 1941).
Hardy, Gathorne, *A Short History of International Affairs*, (London 1939).
Liddell-Hart, Basil, *The Other Side of the Hill*, (London 1948).
Loveday, Arthur, *World War in Spain*, (London 1939).
Madariaga, Salvador de, *Spain*, (New York 1958).
Micaud, Charles, *The French Right and Nazi Germany*, (Duke 1943).
Mowat, Charles Loch-, *Britain Between the Wars*, (London 1955).
Monelli, Paolo, *Mussolini, an Intimate Life*, (London 1953).
Namier, Lewis, *Diplomatic Prelude*, (London 1948);
— *Europe in Decay*, (London 1950).
Peers, Allison, *The Spanish Tragedy*, (London 1936).
Pelling, Henry, *The British Communist Party*, (London 1958).
Reynolds, P. A., *British Foreign Policy in the Inter-War Years*, (London 1954).
Rousseau, Charles, *La Non-Intervention en Espagne*, (Paris 1939).
Schwoeble, Jean, *L'Angleterre et la Sécurité Collective*, (Paris 1938).
Seton-Watson, R. W., *Britain and the Dictators*, (Cambridge 1938).
Steer, G. L., *The Tree of Gernika*, (London 1938).
Stockes, Richard, *Léon Blum, Poet to Premier*, (New York 1937).
Taylor, A. J. P., *The Origins of the Second World War*, (London 1961).
Taylor, F. Jay, *The United States and the Spanish Civil War*, (New York 1956).
Thomas, Hugh, *The Spanish Civil War*, (London 1961).
Times, The History of the, Vol. IV, (London 1952).
"Unknown Diplomat, The," *Britain in Spain*, (London 1939).
Walters, Frank P., *A History of the League of Nations*, Vol. II, (London 1952).
Wellesley, Sir Victor, *Diplomacy in Fetters*, (London 1945).
Werth, Alexander, *The Twilight of France*, (New York 1942).
Wheeler-Bennett, John, *Munich, Prologue to Tragedy*, (London 1948).
Wiskemann, Elizabeth, *The Rome-Berlin Axis*, (London 1949).
Wolfers, Arnold, *Britain and France Between the Wars*, (New York 1940).
Young, George M., *Stanley Baldwin*, (London 1952).

INDEX